Home on the Farm
ON THE
Farm
If Chickens Could Talk

LORENE MCCORMICK BURKHART

Burkhart Network LLC

Published in the United States by Burkhart Network, LLC
4000 N. Meridian Street, Suite 17G
Indianapolis, Indiana 46208
www.loreneburkhart.com

FIRST EDITION

Dust jacket and interior design by
karen kennedy of design in bloom, inc.
www.designinbloominc.com

ISBN-10: 0-9790975-3-3
ISBN-13: 978-0-9790975-3-9

To my parents, their parents, and all of my relatives who blessed me with their love, faith, and courage.

Contents

Preface

When I wrote my autobiography, *An Accidental Pioneer: A Farm Girl's Drive to the Finish ...* the part of the title that seemed to catch the most attention was the word "farm." There's something about farms that attracts peoples' fancies. Perhaps it's the perception that farm life is simpler and more relaxing than city life, or the romantic notion of living "close to the earth."

It's fairly safe to say farm life is simple, I suppose, because responsibilities are clear-cut and never changing. Farm folk do what they must do each day without giving it much thought. The life is far from relaxing, though; farm animals don't have days off, so neither do their keepers. The work is 24/7, 365 days a year, no vacations.

During my childhood in the 1930s and '40s, isolation was also very much a part of farm life. A good half-mile separated us from our nearest neighbor, and it was a seven-mile trip into town over gravel roads, a trip usually made only once a week. My brothers and I learned at early ages to entertain ourselves, a lesson in self-reliance that has served us well throughout our lives.

In this book I have written not a chronology of my childhood years on the farm but rather a series of vignettes, a close-up of special times in my and my family's life. I was not present at several of the events I describe, but I know my family's background and how they lived, and with that knowledge — and some imagination — I put myself in their shoes in an attempt to bring the essence of these wonderful people into their stories. I even went so far as to speculate what my mother's chickens must have thought of us!

I hope you enjoy your "visit" to the farm as much as I have enjoyed giving the "tour."

Lorene McCormick Burkhart
September 2007

Introduction

*L*ife on the farm had a rhythm, the cadence provided daily by the plants and animals we tended. Mornings began with milking and feeding, evenings saw more milking and feeding, plus the gathering of eggs. Adding to this, our lives were filled with the immediacy of the seasons. From early spring to late fall, crops were planted and harvested, gardens were tended and the food they produced processed for use during the cold months. Quiet time came only during the winter when the land slept beneath its coverlets of frost and snow.

This rhythm of life created a sense of security that counterbalanced the insecure and too-often erratic rhythm of unpredictable weather that could destroy a season's crops and diseases that could decimate a flock or herd. The land and animals that were the essence of the farm added to our security, but with that came also the knowledge that we in turn needed to support them. Cropland was nothing more than barren field until it was sown; cattle, sheep, pigs, and chickens could provide food only if they were also provided for.

The men worked in the fields from dawn to dusk and returned home exhausted. The women were often weary from their unrelenting chores; even their "sit-down" time was filled with mending and darning.

1

Children absorbed this rhythm and cycle, trusting that adults would find a way to make everything work. Breakfast would be on the table every morning, the bus would come around the corner to take them to their classes on school days, and jars and jars of food would line the basement shelves each winter.

It was our life and it seemed right. Couples married, babies were born, and old folks died. And always there was a pattern, a purpose.

Each of the chapters in this book is in essence a story unto itself, a description of a certain time or event of my life on the farm. Because the kitchen was the heart and soul of the household, I've added many of my family's favorite recipes to spice things up. Memories were more often than not made and delivered over the stove.

As you look into the windows of our lives, I hope you will catch a glimmer of the honesty and truth that were our core, and the steadfastness and courage that were our foundation.

It was a good life.

CHAPTER 1

Cluck, cluck, cluck

It was late afternoon, just after four. The sun was getting low in the summer sky when we heard the gate to our chicken yard open. Here came the Girl, ambling toward the henhouse, egg basket over her arm and acting like she didn't have a care in the world, just as she did every day around this time. One look at her face, though, told us it was all too clear that she did care, and that she wasn't very happy about coming to see us. For that matter, we weren't all that happy to see her!

"What do you think, Mama Hen?" Callie Cluck asked. "Will she poke us with that stick when she reaches under us to get our eggs today?"

As People go — at least the ones we knew, those who lived in the House next to our yard — she wasn't very big, a little blond-haired thing with legs almost as skinny and knobby as ours. But she could be so mean, or so we thought. She usually acted like we were something to be afraid of, little birds that we are, and often brought a stick that she poked us with to stir us off our nests. We didn't like being disturbed there in the first place, but oh, how we hated that stick and we pecked at her whenever she stuck it at us. Maybe that's what made us "scary" to her.

Grandma Biddie had been around longer than the rest of us, and said more than once that she never felt quite as comfortable when the Girl collected our eggs as she did when the Lady, the Girl's mother, did. The Lady was much more gentle and talked to us in low, soothing tones as she went from nest to nest, and she never brought a stick. We still didn't like the reach and grab, but we rarely pecked at her, and if we did she just took it in stride.

"But of course," Grandma rationalized, feathers ruffling, "the Lady has been gathering eggs much longer than the Girl has, so it's easier for her."

"Whatever," Aunt Bantie said. "Still, I think the Lady is nicer to us because she wants us to be happy. I've heard her tell that chick of hers that 'a happy hen equals a happy egg.' "

Randy Rooster strutted into the henhouse around then and poked his beak into the conversation, as he always did, the showoff! According to him, dawn isn't dawn, nor is any conversation worth having, until he's put his two-crows'-worth in.

"Happy egg, happy egg," he squawked. "The People don't care about your being happy. All they wants is the eggs, you silly clucks. A happy *rooster* is what makes a happy barnyard. Without me, your lives would be empty, meaningless — and eggless!"

We had to agree that Randy had his worth. For one thing, he seemed to know how to keep the Girl in line. He'd peck around, seemingly minding his own business, but watching for her to come into our yard. Then he would chase her around with his neck stretched out and his feathers all a-fluff, which made him look bigger and fiercer than he really was. Every now and then she'd be ready for him and clip him with a kick. How we would laugh to see him tumble and run squawking, even though he wasn't hurt at all. The Girl knew better than to do any more than scare him enough to him shoo him off; he was too valuable to her mother's egg business. Randy knew she knew that, and that made him even bolder. So, with a shake of his tail, he was out of the henhouse and off to strut his stuff.

The Girl came cautiously in, eyeing us as warily as we were her. Whether or not we would peck her hands depended on whether she had the hated stick. To our relief, she had not brought it. "Let's be nice to her today," Grandma said, shifting slightly to one side so the Girl could get reach under her easily, "and maybe she won't ever bring the stick again."

"Well, let's not let her off too easily," Aunt Bantie grumbled, although the quick peck she gave the Girl was a more-gentle-than-usual nip. Before long our nests were empty, the basket was full, and the Girl was on her way back to the House.

Shortly afterward the rumble of a truck motor and the crunch of heavy tires on the gravel drive told us that the man from the feed store had come to make his weekly delivery. "Oh my," Callie sighed. "Just *look* at all that lovely chicken feed." We saw a few bags of ground oyster shells being unloaded too.

"I can't tell that our food tastes any better with that stuff mixed in," Callie remarked. "What's the point?"

Grandma, who was wiser than all of us, said, "I heard the Girl ask her mother that once, and the Lady said it added something called 'calcium' to our diets, and that makes our eggshells stronger." Well, that was amazing, we thought. A few of us remembered times when the shells of our eggs weren't very strong and they broke in our nests. What a

5

mess! "Also," Grandma continued, "eggs with strong shells sell better, the Lady said."

That last remark got us thinking. Every day we laid eggs, and every day the People took them away. It seemed like a strange routine to us, but that was our job and we really didn't mind. Our lovely eggs made the Lady and the Girl happy, and what else did we have to do anyway?

Still, we wondered. One day every week the Lady carefully set crates full of our eggs in the trunk of her car and drove off with them, and each time she came back with a satisfied smile. "I sold them for a good price today," she would say, and the Girl would hop and dance for joy because that good price usually meant pretty fabric for a new dress for her.

"Oh, but I just love it when she wears the feedbag dresses the Lady makes for her," Aunt Biddie said, and we all clucked in agreement. The feed-bag material had lovely prints indeed; the Lady was very clever and the dresses she made for the Girl were quite attractive. Besides, seeing the Girl in something that brought nice thoughts of yummy food made having her visits to us less unpleasant whenever she brought that awful stick.

The sun was setting lower in the sky, and we preened our feathers and settled further down into our nests, talking a bit more about the People. What interesting creatures they were, always busy about this and that. We observed them carefully whenever we were out in the yard pecking around for bugs and pebbles. The Man didn't seem to be around much at all except for a couple of days a week, and the Boys were usually around and about whatever business they had on other parts of the farm. It was the Lady and the Girl we knew the best, and even they had so much more to do than taking care of us: hanging laundry on high lines in our yard and working in the garden nearby. Many summer days found the Girl picking fruit out of the cherry tree in the corner of our yard, a task she didn't seem to mind. We didn't mind it either because she always dropped a few here and there and we'd gobble them up. Yummy!

When the Boys did come into the chicken yard we didn't appreciate their visits. They always brought a large, round orange thing that they bounced back and forth, running around, bumping into each other, jumping and leaping and tossing the orange thing into a hoop with some netting that had been mounted on a tall post in the center of the space. Usually just the two big Boys participated in this strange activity, but sometimes they'd let the little one join in. Regardless of how many of them were there, we did our best to stay far out of their way. Just the thought of that bouncy thing landing on us was enough to make us shudder.

Other things the People did really made us shudder even more, though, like when the Lady would take a couple of young pullets from the brooder house located across the yard from our henhouse — poor things! — and hang them by their feet from a clothesline where she'd cut off their heads. We couldn't bear to watch.

"And what about what they do then?" Aunt Bantie once asked. "They say they're 'dressing' it, but it seems more to me that they are *undressing* those innocent youngsters!"

We nodded our heads and clucked softly in sympathy. We egg-layers pretty much kept to ourselves (it doesn't pay to get too close to someone who was going to end up on a dinner table the next day) but still we felt sorry for those poor souls from the brooder house who would never know the joy of laying a nestful of eggs, even if the People did take them away as fast as we could pop them out.

The sky was now a lovely shade of pale violet with a pink-red-orange streak lighting up the west. We were as sleepy as chickens can be, and anyone who has "gone to bed with the chickens" knows we go to bed early. Grandma's head had been tucked under her wing for some time now — the old seem to need more sleep — and by the time darkness fell the rest of us were sound asleep too, feathers fluffed to keep us warm and getting our much-needed rest. Dawn would come before we knew it. Randy's cock-a-doodle-doo would wake us, and the People too. Another day would break, and once more we would take our place in the pecking order of the farm.

CHAPTER 2

Baking Biscuits and Other Kitchen Therapy

*W*hat is it about working with our hands that, when troubles plague us, offers just the sense of detachment we need to sort through our problems and find peace again? Men often will tinker around in their garage or basement workshops or take the car engine apart. Many women find therapy in knitting, crocheting, or playing the piano.

The women in my family also cooked.

My grandmother and mother and aunts spent countless hours in the kitchen, and as I recall, they were for the most part a pretty contented bunch. For them, cooking and baking went beyond being just a chore, a task to see to every day. It was an art, a craft they took pride in, one they worked hard daily to improve upon.

My mother was an outstanding cook who intuitively knew how to put a batch of ingredients together and turn out a masterpiece every time. Mind you, I say this not from daughterly loyalty: Knox County, Indiana, abounded with testimony on

Mother's superb culinary skills. And my brothers will cheerfully disagree with anyone who challenges that.

That's not to say that she didn't have her less-than-successful moments. Case in point: When my parents were young newlyweds, Emma (my mother) decided one morning to surprise and please her young husband, Clarence (Dad), by making biscuits for his breakfast. Biscuits were, after all, a breakfast mainstay in most farm kitchens but they had not been part of the morning menu in her childhood home and she had never made them. Undaunted, though, as she was skilled in baking, she figured, How hard could it be? Throw together some flour, baking powder, salt, shortening, and milk; stir it up, roll it out on the oilcloth-covered tabletop, cut out the circles, and put them on a pan. Pop them in the oven, bake until golden brown, and serve the tender morsels to her appreciative bridegroom. Nothing to it.

The morsels were anything but tender. In fact, as she laughingly described them in later years, "They were hard as rocks!"

This baking disaster clearly didn't damage the relationship; Mother and Dad's marriage lasted almost sixty years, until his death in January 1983, and the tale of the biscuit fiasco became one of Mother's favorite stories.

What she hadn't realized at the time, despite the seeming simplicity of making biscuits, was that less was more, and the light fluffiness that constitutes a good biscuit needed more attention to technique than she gave it. For instance, a *very* gentle touch while mixing, kneading, and rolling is essential. When biscuit dough is mistreated, it rebels — much like humans.

Mother didn't give up on making biscuits altogether, but they were never her forte. No one missed them, though, because she made so many other yummy baked goods. You name it, she could make it. You might say she was a "natural" in the pastry department (although I never heard of the word "pastry" until it was introduced years later in one of my home economics classes).

%. %. %. %. %.

In my childhood years on the farm, grocery stores offered no such convenience items like ready-made pies and cake mixes. A farm wife had to be at least competent, if not downright adept, in the kitchen to properly feed her family. The women in my family were no exception, and home-baked goods were the order of almost every day, if not in our own oven, then in those of my Grandma and aunts Helen, Lilly, Dorothy, Edna, or Midah. These women were not just bakers; they were *bakers*!

My aunts and Grandma have been gone for many years now, but when I think back to the culinary wonders they created, I can almost smell and taste them. My mouth waters, my stomach growls, and I get all misty-eyed. But I wonder sometimes: Were they really as good as I remember? Or is it the memory and the mystique that made them so special?

Everyone no doubt has their own "kitchen memories," recollections of foods we loved that were family traditions as we were growing up. In my seven-plus decades of life I have reached an age of perception and perspective — that is, I'm old enough to reflect on my family members' various personality quirks and behaviors that often accompanied kitchen activity.

Pies, cakes, cookies, and sometimes homemade bread were as certain on the kitchen table (or the dining table, if company was coming) as Sunday arriving every week.

And speaking of Sunday — now, that was really special because that's when we had "Sunday cake," which was fancier than "everyday cake." Once I turned ten, it was frequently my job to bake the dessert offerings for my family. I felt so grown up, like I had joined the ranks of the family bakers. The cakes I made were part of my 4-H projects and my earlier endeavors came from the basic recipes in the Baking I and II booklets from 4-H — beginner cakes, in other words. My brothers, used to Mother's wonderful confections, grumbled when presented with standard yellow and white cakes week after week. Were they ever relieved when I moved on to more advanced baking and the cakes got fancier and better.

When it came to Sunday deserts, however, my aunt Helen reigned supreme with her stunning Lady Baltimore cake. Studded throughout with maraschino cherries (a real treat for me because we never had such "exotic" items in our own home pantry) and crowned with piles of fluffy seven-minute frosting, the cake was Aunt Helen's pride and joy.

Lady Baltimores were Aunt Helen's and Aunt Helen's alone. There was, no doubt, a sense of competition among the women in our farm community as to who made the best pickles, who baked the best pies, and who could turn out the most beautiful cakes. That competitive spirit existed in my family also, but when one clearly outshone the others in a particular area, they bowed to her expertise. It was an unspoken law: Each woman had her own specialty, one she was known for, and that turf was not to be trod upon by the others. Heaven help a transgressor!

In our own little immediate family enclave, though, my brothers and I treasured my mother's "special-day" cake tradition, a tall, lighter-than-air angel food, a delectable delight made only for birthdays. I discovered in my adulthood that her recipe came straight from the Swans Down cake flour box, but even with that knowledge, to her children it remains *her* specialty, exquisite in its simplicity, decorated with nothing more than a plain powdered-sugar, vanilla, and milk icing. (Frosting was not in my vocabulary until later, either.) When I was little, I loved "helping" Mother ice the cake because afterward she let me scrape the bowl for any remaining sugar mixture that might be clinging to the sides.

To this day I remember the tantalizing fragrance of that cake as it baked in the oven. Getting it out of the pan required a measure of skill; the pan needed to be carefully turned upside-down and balanced by the center tube on a coffee cup to allow the cake to cool. Finally it would be ready to be tapped out of the pan. "Lorene, get the cake plate from the china cupboard," she would say, but I was already on my way back to the kitchen with it before the last word was out of her mouth. She would slide a long knife around the edges to loosen the cake from the pan and then, as I held my breath, gently turn it out onto the waiting plate. Perfect!

A few crusty pieces always stuck to the sides of the cake pan and my little brother Eddie and I would attack those with a spoon. I don't know what it was about bits and pieces stuck to pans and bowls, but they were divine, almost as wonderful as the finished product.

As my baking skills improved through my 4-H years I became confident and was ready to tackle complicated recipes. One year I decided to enter my Hungarian coffee cake for competition at the Knox County Fair. The cake came out alright but it wasn't holding together very well and I had my doubts about its arriving at the fair intact. While Mother drove the fourteen miles to the fairgrounds in Bicknell, I held

Kitchen Prayer

Lord of all pots and pans and things,
Since I've no time to be
A Saint by doing lovely deeds
Or watching late with Thee
Or dreaming in the dawnlight
Or storming Heaven's gates,
Make me a saint by getting meals
and washing up the plates!

Although I must have Martha's hands,
I have a Mary mind;
And when I black the boots and shoes,
Thy sandals, Lord, I find!
I think of how they trod the earth,
What time I scrub the floor;
Accept this meditation, Lord!
I haven't time for more.

Warm all the kitchen with thy love,
And light it with thy peace!
Forgive me all my worrying,
And make my grumbling cease!
Thou who didst love to give men food,
In a room or by the seas;
Accept this service that I do —
I do it unto Thee!

— author unknown

14

my breath and held my hands around the cake the entire time. Somehow, whether by the power of positive thinking or the heat from my hands, the cake was perfectly stuck together by the time we arrived. I received a Grand Champion award for my efforts, and later, at the State Fair, a blue ribbon. I had arrived!

※ ※ ※ ※ ※

June came around, sometimes rainy, often dusty. But late May and early June marked the beginning of strawberry season, which was always a special time. A nearby neighbor had what was called a "sand farm" with the kind of loose, sandy soil that was ideal for growing strawberries and melons. When the berries ripened in that brief space of time just before the real summer set in, Mother would drive over and come home with a twenty-four-quart crate of them purchased from the neighbor, and then the fun began.

The arrival of the strawberries was almost like a holiday. Because they kept only a few days our whole work routine would change to accommodate processing the fruit.

A flurry of activity ensued. The berries were washed, stemmed, lightly sugared, and placed gently in one-quart plastic freezer containers. When the lids were snapped into place, the boxes were stacked into baskets and transported to a frozen-food locker we had in town, seven miles from our farm, where we also kept other fruits and meat.

The locker stop was always last on the agenda when we went into town on Saturdays. We would select whatever we needed for the week, then go home and store it in the freezer section of our refrigerator; the compartment was small so we had to plan carefully. In the 1950s, we bought a deep freeze that we kept in our enclosed back porch and she really became creative with the strawberries. A few quarts usually became "freezer strawberry jam," a runny mixture that also served well as an ice cream topping.

Not every berry went into the freezer, though, and during the all-too-brief time we had them fresh we enjoyed another of Mother's baking traditions: strawberry shortcake, always made with sponge cake instead of biscuits. I think she simply didn't want to deal with biscuits.

Mother seemed to be affected by the fruit seasons, and her moods always seemed to match how her preferences ran. If her taste was leaning more toward strawberries rather than peaches, she was happier during strawberry season and we could look forward to shortcakes and jams till our sides split. If peaches ranked higher, we knew pies and cobblers would be on the menu for some time. Didn't matter to us. We loved them all.

Applesauce time also seemed to be a hit with Mother. I didn't particularly share her rosy attitude, though, and my mood was definitely not at its peak at that production time. When I saw the baskets of early green apples on the back-porch counter, I knew it was time to haul all of the dusty Ball canning jars up from the cellar. That in itself wasn't so bad, but before we could scrub them in the porch sink and sterilize them, I had to evict all the bugs that had crawled into the jars and died during the winter, which wasn't my idea of a pleasant task.

How did the apples become applesauce? These little hands can tell the tale of bushel after bushel of apples to be washed, cored, and cut into fourths. Into the cooking pot they went where they simmered until soft; it was then time for them to come back to me, and I was READY!

A funnel-shaped aluminum colander stood on three tall, skinny legs over a big crock. The hot apples were ladled into the colander and I forced the mixture through the holes in its sides with a conical wooden pestle, thus separating out the peels. Once that was done liberal quantities of sugar and cinnamon were added. My nose still tickles when I think of that tantalizing spicy fragrance.

The actual canning process required meticulous attention to ladling just the right amount of applesauce into the jars, applying the lids, and pressure-cooking the jars to seal them. A bad seal meant spoiled applesauce, a waste of both produce and labor. Mother therefore saw to those last tasks herself, not allowing me to even help, so to this day I couldn't can anything to save my life.

For that matter, I'm perfectly happy not knowing how to can. I swore when I left the farm home food processing "plant" that I would never press another apple through a colander or place another peach half in a wide-mouthed jar so it overlapped the others "just so." No pressure cooker has ever darkened my kitchen door!

%. %. %. %. %.

Pies hold a special place in my heart. Cherry, apple, peach, blackberry — they all were a little slice of heaven. Fruit pies tended to have enough substance that you could, if you didn't mind sticky fingers, pick them up in your hand and eat them, thus earning the categorization of "hand pies." Fluffier and more delicate cream pies that could be eaten only with a fork were called "plate pie."

My aunt Edna was the best plate pie maker in our universe, and when Uncle Ray would roll up the driveway in his "pick'em up truck" (his favorite mode of transportation)

on our birthdays, we knew he was bringing the best present of all: our choice of coconut cream, banana cream, chocolate cream, or lemon meringue. It was all we kids could do to keep from falling on the pie and devouring it right there in the gravel driveway, but we restrained ourselves, thanking Uncle Ray and nodding solemnly at his admonition to be sure to return the pie plate for the next lucky recipient. (Not that anyone could avoid that; all careful farm wives made sure to write their "return to" name on a piece of adhesive tape attached to the bottom outside of the plate.) Besides, we knew that sharing Aunt Edna's birthday pies with loved ones was almost as good as receiving them.

Other everyday favorites at our home included apple crisp, a stand-in when time was too short for making a pie. Served with a dip of vanilla ice cream on top, it was hard to beat! But my own all-time favorite "comfort food" was bread pudding. Mother always made it when I came home from college because she knew my passion for it. It was always served plain, without sauce, and even if Mother had made sauce for it, I can guarantee it would never have had whiskey in it because liquor was taboo in our home.

A Thanksgiving and Christmas treat was Mother's date pudding. Dense and dark, served up with the rich, sweet sauce that formed in the bottom of the pan while it was baking and a mound of whipped cream — lots of whipped cream, in my case — it was a holiday carol unto itself. (I still remember my dad saying to me, "Lorene, would you like some date pudding with your whipped cream?")

Mother was a culinary creature of habit, and date pudding was made at no other time of the year, not New Year's, not Easter, just Thanksgiving and Christmas. Begging

Hard-as-rocks biscuits didn't put a dent in my parents' relationship. They enjoyed almost sixty years together as husband and wife.

and pleading would have done no good, she made things when she made them. Period.

The same principle applied to hermits, cookies that Mother and her sisters Lilly and Helen made only at Christmastime. There was nothing particularly Christmassy about hermits; they were slightly crunchy cookies, moist, spicy, and nutty, with a hint of orange. Each woman made a six-dozen batch in early December, and those had to last throughout the season because when they were gone, they were gone. No more would be made. Mother always hid the hermits to keep us kids from raiding them, but to no avail. We found them anyway. That was part of the magic, part of what made them so special: the hiding, the hunting and raiding, and trying not to go through them too fast because it would be another year before we had them again.

Aunt Lilly was a real whiz in the kitchen and made the most wonderful peanut butter cookies. My cousin Imo inherited her recipes and one day, as we reminisced about those cookies, she produced the recipe and shared it with me so that I can enjoy them whenever I get the whim.

Another standout in our home was chocolate chip cookies. When Nestle's Toll House chocolate chips debuted at the local A&P we could hardly wait to try the cookie recipe on the back of the package. It remained a favorite until a Chicago friend of Mother's sent her a recipe for chocolate chip oatmeal cookies, which were so yummy the Nestle's recipe was quickly abandoned. As my brothers and I married and left home, Mother's cookies were the first thing we wanted when we stepped in the back door for a visit. We'd make a beeline for her aluminum cookie can with the word "cookies" written on the lid that always sat on the countertop between the sink and the stove.

Grandma McCormick's signature cookies were sugar cookies. A batch was always available in the "safe" in the pantry. I didn't have too many opportunities to eat them at Grandma's because she died when I was about ten years old, but Aunt Midah, her oldest daughter, carried on the tradition, so I enjoyed them whenever I visited her house.

%. %. %. %. %.

When holidays came around, the grandparents' home tended to be the center of activity. My mother's parents died before I was born, so we usually spent Thanksgiving, Christmas, and Easter with Dad's side of the family.

An Easter favorite was Aunt Dorothy's Parker House rolls — small, golden, yeasty pillows folded over in the middle, leaving a perfect pocket for home-churned butter. She rose at dawn to make the dough so there would be enough time to let it rise until it was doubled, at which time she'd punch it down. The rising and punching was repeated once more, then she'd pinch off pieces to make the rolls. Then off to Grandma's Aunt Dorothy and her family went, and by the time they arrived the rolls had finished their final rise and were ready to pop into the oven.

On other occasions, Aunt Midah often made Huxley rolls. Both hers and Aunt Dorothy's were melt-in-your-mouth scrumptious, especially with homemade jelly.

※ ※ ※ ※ ※

The kitchen was without doubt the hub of farm families, the place not only for cooking and eating, but also the social center of the home. Meals were enjoyed as a family, and no one rushed away from the table because he or she might have "something better" to do. Surprisingly, though, despite all the delicious and plentiful food, farm folks back then were seldom overweight, no doubt because all their hard work used up the calories they consumed. Ingredients were definitely more wholesome than many found nowadays, and meals were well balanced and healthy because of the wide variety of homegrown fruits and vegetables served at each one. Between-meal snacks were almost unheard of — with

Out of the kitchen: (from left) Aunt Lilly, Aunt Helen, and Mother.

so much work to be done, who had the time for that? My parents' snacking was usually limited to the "bite" of dessert they enjoyed at the end of their meals.

My sons are grown and gone and I now live alone, so I don't cook or bake as much as I used to, but I still enjoy breaking in a new recipe or revitalizing an old one. I more often than not give away the fruits of my labors, but I don't mind. It just feels good doing it.

My cousins and I have many of the family recipes and we whip some of them up whenever we have the time and the inclination. But it always seems like something is a bit "off" or not quite as we remembered it from our childhood. Maybe it's because we're using different pans, different ovens. Maybe things were not as good as we thought they were.

Or maybe it's because they're missing the chief ingredient: the love that went into each and every one.

CHAPTER 3

Aunt Lilly

Summer 1909

*L*illy shifted the infant, her little brother Robert, in her arms a bit, listening to what the minister was saying. She blinked back the tears that stung her eyes and studied the faces of the others who stood at the graveside. The oldest brothers, fifteen-year-old Clarence and Oscar, twelve, were trying to be strong and manly but their red eyes and noses belied them. The little boys, Gilbert and Raymond, six and four respectively, didn't try so hard to be brave and clung to the skirts of their older sisters Selma and Helen, who wept softly. Lilly gave them a small smile of encouragement. Selma, at age fourteen, had already proven an invaluable help and support. Helen was only ten, but she had grown up fast in the three days since Mama died.

Lilly herself had needed to grow up at an early age. As the firstborn of a family of nine children, she had acted as a second mother to her sisters and brothers for years. Now seventeen, she was more than capable of taking care of the brood and the house as well as her mother had. What would be missing was her mother's advice and encouragement, and her love.

As miserable as she was feeling, though, the pain and bewilderment on her father's face tore at her heart. August Bobe had always thought that he and his wife would grow old together, watching their children have families of their own. But having nine children in eighteen years can take a heavy toll on even the strongest woman, and at only forty-three years of age Anna Sophia's heart had given out, just three months after little Robert's birth.

As the family turned away from the grave and started toward the wagon that would take them home, baby Robert began to fuss. Aunt Louise patted Lilly's arm. "I'll take him now, dear," she said, and Lilly regretfully handed the baby to her. Much discussion had gone on in the past two days and it was decided that Aunt Lou and Uncle John, August's brother, who had no children of their own, would take Robert and raise him in town. He was a sweet baby and Lilly loved him dearly, but she finally had been forced to admit that caring for a young infant along with the rest of the family would be more than she could manage.

Lilly felt a tug at her sleeve, and looked down into the sad crystal-blue eyes of her little sister Emma. Only seven years old, she had always been a quiet, solemn child, and was even more so now. "Lilly," Emma said, sniffling, "what's going to happen to us?"

"I don't know exactly, Emmy," Lilly said, putting her arm around the little girl and giving her a hug. "But as long as we're together, we'll get along just fine."

※ ※ ※ ※ ※

And the family did get along just fine. The Bobes were of strong stock, and the words "quit" and "give up" were not part of their vocabulary. August's parents had endured a long ocean voyage when they emigrated from Prussia in the northern area of Germany in 1852, resolutely overcoming language and cultural barriers after disembarking in New Orleans, and working their way north to settle in Knox County in southwestern Indiana. Anna Sophia Vollmer's family, also immigrants, had been cut from a similar sturdy cloth.

August, born in 1867, was the ninth of eleven children, so the tending of a large family in itself was not daunting for him. He was a good manager and he was blessed with good, hardworking children, which was fortunate indeed because not only did the youngsters have farm and household work, they also were expected to assist with the family business, tending the cows of the Bobe Dairy and processing the milk they produced. The family's primary source of income came from selling the milk in Vincennes, delivered door-to-door to customers by August in his horse-drawn wagon.

Lilly was by nature a "mother hen," a good thing since she and Selma had their hands full with the never-ending cycle of cooking, canning, gardening, cleaning, and laundry. Farm work was hard on the family's clothing, so there was always a pile of sewing and mending that needed to be done as well. By the time all the chores were done and the youngsters put to bed, there was little time for socializing. The girls fell exhausted into their beds at night, talking a bit and sharing dreams, happy just to be together.

The years passed and the children began to grow into young adults. They got their education at the one-room school about a half-mile from their home, all going only through eighth grade. All but Helen, that is, who had the opportunity to go to high school in Vincennes and become a teacher. (Little Robert, raised as an only child by his doting uncle and aunt, was privileged enough to not only go to college but also medical school. His promising future was cut short, however, when he died of an apparent congenital heart defect at age twenty-nine.)

The little ones grew into big ones and moved away, starting families of their own. August never remarried, and Lilly and Selma remained at the home place with him. A quiet but contented trio they were until one night Selma awoke with agonizing pain in her belly. The local doctor did what he could, but it was of no use and the young woman died hours later of peritonitis from a ruptured appendix. She was only thirty-one.

August grieved at the loss of his beloved daughter, but Lilly was devastated. She and Selma, having been through so much together, were so close it almost seemed that they shared the same thoughts. For Lilly, a part of her soul had been torn away.

She worked through her sorrow by keeping busy, especially with her much-loved sewing and needlecraft — embroidery, crocheting, and tatting were popular in those days — and her favorite pastime, her flower garden. She was an unusually intelligent woman who often quoted the poetry learned while attending the little country school. Lilly was a happy person by nature, and her cheerful demeanor was a joy to everyone around her. She never owned an automobile and never learned to drive one, choosing instead to depend on friends and neighbors to provide transportation for shopping, going to church, and visiting family. Perhaps learning to drive was not of interest to her because she preferred passing the time spent on errands talking and just being with those she loved.

※ ※ ※ ※ ※

My aunt Lilly remained what in those days was called a spinster and stayed at the family homestead, even after my grandfather's death in November of 1932 of injuries he suffered a few weeks earlier when he was attacked by a bull. It may be that, having raised her siblings and helping out with their children, she didn't need a family of her own. The closest she came to that was when she took her nephew Bob to live with her when his mother became unable to care for him.

As a child, I never gave much thought to how special Aunt Lilly was. She was just Aunt Lilly. She was always available to stay and take care of us any time Mother had to be away, and we all were used to having her around at Sunday dinners and at family reunions, where she would always bring one of her marvelous dishes. The family knew they had a treasure in her, a real culinary jewel. What they didn't know was that others far beyond the family circle also knew of Lilly's talents.

Aunt Lilly had developed a reputation for her kitchen skills, and word had traveled as far as America's Southwest. How this happened, I don't know, but in the late 1940s she worked several years for Barry Goldwater's household in Arizona. The home fires called to her, though, and she returned to Indiana where she was put in charge of the cafeteria of a grade school near Vincennes. The children ate well and even the teachers praised the wonderful food, leaving the principal at a loss to understand how they could enjoy such delightful meals every day and still make a profit!

Always lovely, always smiling: that was my aunt Lilly.

May 31 - 1942

Keep your heart free from
hate, your mind from worry,
Live simply; expect little;
give much; fill your heart
with love; scatter sunshine.
Forget self. Think of others;
and do as you would be
done by.
        Love
            Aunt Lil.

A note Aunt Lilly wrote to me, offering words to live by.

As clever with her finances as she was with food, by the time she returned to Indiana, independent Lilly had managed to save enough money to purchase her own homes, first one in Vincennes and a later another one a couple of miles out of town. Her legendary flower gardens went with her, always started from scratch with seeds and "starts" from friends and family. Summer days would find her in the back of the house where the cutting gardens were located, clipping blooms for bouquets for church and shut-ins.

Aunt Lilly spent her entire lifetime serving others, but she was never subservient. Lilly Bobe was a strong woman with a mind of her own who did what she wanted to do. She died in 1967 at age seventy-five, but it wasn't until several years later that I began to fully understand and appreciate what a remarkable person she was. I had been lucky enough to inherit her carefully preserved files filled with all kinds of household tips and recipes clipped from newspapers and magazines, and as I went through them I discovered to my surprise how much like her I am, always clipping and filing, dreaming about flower gardens I wish I had the time to grow and whipping up tasty meals out of almost nothing.

It's a shame it takes the perspective of growing older ourselves to realize how much we loved and appreciated someone who's gone. But is it ever too late to tell them how we feel? True, it's always better to do so when that dear one is still living, but I try to express my love for my aunt Lilly by trying to be like her and remembering her in my prayers. She had a lot of experience with young children and their concern for nothing beyond the next day, but she was the very soul of patience, and I'm sure she knows how I feel and didn't mind waiting to hear it from me. I sure hope so.

CHAPTER 4

Emma,
the Business Woman

*T*he two chickens hung upside-down by their feet from the clothesline, limply flapping occasionally like rags in the summer breeze, but for the most part just limp, seemingly resigned to their fate. Mother approached each one. Whack-whack went her butcher knife, and plop-plop went the heads into the dusty yard below.

Having been pecked many times by chickens while gathering eggs, I didn't especially like them, and as Mother went about her task it never occurred to me to feel sorry for the birds. Still, I winced with each whack, avoiding the sight of the flopping, headless carcass as long as I could, and was always grateful that Mother never expected me to take over this particular chore.

My own part was hard enough as it was. Once the whacked chickens stopped their flopping, they were taken down from the line and brought to me. I was in charge of a large bucket of boiling water, into which I dipped the birds for a few moments to loosen their feathers. When they were cool enough to touch, I pulled out the feathers, then held the carcasses briefly over a fire in our trash-burning barrel, which loosened the stubborn pinfeathers that remained lodged in the skins.

At this point, I handed them back to Mother, and she would complete dressing the critters and getting them ready for the skillet. As I worked, though, I couldn't help but think back to when these chickens first came to our farm.

%% %% %% %% %%

Some distance from our hen houses, where our egg-layers lived, we had a brooder house, a small wooden structure about twelve feet square that was intended as a heated abode for baby chicks. It had two doors, one big enough for people to come and go, and one just for chicks that opened onto two side-by-side garden plots. (Access to these plots was alternated from year to year, the idea being that the chicks' droppings would fertilize the plots; it wouldn't do, however, for one particular plot to become "over-fertilized.")

Every year, the first week in March brought a bustle of activity as the brooder house was cleaned, the heaters that kept the baby chicks warm were checked and made operational, and the glass water jars and grain feeders were cleaned and ready to be filled.

Finally, the big day arrived. I could hardly wait to get home from school to see the tiny arrivals — they were so cute, like little fluffy toys. Mother always ordered five hundred chicks, which she brought home from the hatchery in cardboard flats, twenty-four-inches square by eight inches high with two-inch holes in the sides for ventilation, and carried into the brooder house. So much chirping greeted us when the lid was lifted — along with the pungent aroma of their droppings. The babies, no more than three inches high, were carefully taken out of the box and gently placed onto the warmed cement floor, where they toddled around, bumping into and tumbling over each other while they inspected their new quarters. Mother and I couldn't help but laugh at their awkward antics.

I enjoyed helping out with them, which gave me a chance to scoop the little birds up in my hands and play with them a bit. It was Mother, however, who was truly the "Mother Hen" for the chicks, the mistress of the brooder house. She made sure their feeders and water bottles were kept full (even if it was I who did the filling), that the house was kept just the right temperature and that the chicks didn't escape into the chill of the early spring winds and rains.

Toward mid-April the weather warmed up enough and the chicks' downy fluff had turned to more insulating feathers, and it was time for them to come out into the world. I propped open the door leading to the garden plot and watched. The birds clustered near the door and looked out, blinking at the bright sunlight. This was something new, and they were confused, unsure what to do, cheeping their bewilderment.

Finally, one brave soul stepped to the door and stuck his head out, then perched on the threshold and stood there a moment, cocking his head this way and that. Tentatively he stepped out into the yard. This wasn't so bad! What's that — food? Peck. Nope, a rock. Peck. A bug, yum. Peck by peck he ventured farther, and eventually the others followed, drawn both by curiosity and the fact that nothing bad had happened to their leader. Each day they became more courageous, nibbling more of the bugs and grass and requiring less of the expensive "indoor" feed. Come nighttime they were herded back into the brooder house where they would be protected from foxes, coyotes, and other predators.

Mother took good care of her chickens. This was no idle hobby, after all. All year long Mother sold the eggs gathered from our laying hens, and when the brooder-house chickens reached sufficient weight for eating, they too would be sold or go onto our own dinner table. The chicks Mother bought every year were an investment, and she intended to get a return on the hard-earned money she had paid for them. Accounts on the birds were kept as meticulously as those for the rest of the farm; every bit of grain pecked up, as well as every chick that died before reaching maturity, which happened often, was tracked. In time, several of the youngsters would be added to our egg-laying group and the qualifying eggs from them (intact and of proper weight) were sold to the hatchery, where they would become the next brood of baby chickens, starting the cycle all over again.

By July the chicks reached adulthood, no longer cute babies but mature gray leghorns; the drab-looking hens were definitely outshone by their rooster companions who strutted fancily around the yard, flipping their combs and waving their long tail plumes as they pursued each romantic conquest. In their bird-brained ignorance, life was pretty pleasant for these two-pound pullets, and ignorance truly was bliss for them, considering that most of them by now had pending dates with an iron skillet.

To the chickens, people had always been a source of food, nothing to be afraid of, so Mother had no problems walking into the brooder-house yard, grabbing up a couple of fryers by the legs, one bird in each hand, and hauling them off, squawking, to the clothesline. You know how the rest of that story goes.

After I cleaned the chickens and handed them off, I never hung around to watch while Mother pulled out the innards and cut the birds into frying pieces. I came to regret this when I became a bride because buying a whole chicken and cutting it up myself would have been by far much cheaper than getting one already cut up, and I could have saved my young family quite a bit of money.

At least I had learned how to fry a chicken — and from the master! That often became my chore once I was old enough to take it over, although even then we often shared the task, she dredging the pieces in her special blend of flour, salt, and pepper, then passing them to me to snuggle into the sizzling fat awaiting in the huge iron skillet. Mother never had to call anyone twice for dinner. The aroma of the crispy, golden poultry and its companion mashed potatoes and gravy drew the diners promptly. No one ever tired of Mother's wonderful fried chicken, and I have never, ever tasted any as good as hers — not even my own. It's just not the same.

% % % % %

Some might think we were heartless, to take adorable-looking chicks only to raise them to be eaten. Those folks never lived on a farm.

It's not that my family and other farmers didn't like animals. They did, and took good care of them, but there was no room for sentimentality. The animals were not pets. They were a commodity, as much a part of the business of farming as the sowing and growing of corn, hay, and alfalfa. Even dogs and cats had clear-cut responsibilities, to ward off predators and keep vermin under control; they neither expected nor got special status.

I'm sure my mother never considered herself a business woman, but she was. I recall her sitting at the kitchen table at night with the checkbook, bills, and accounting book laid out before her. Granted, the only pies that graced our kitchen were edible ones and not on charts. Still, Mother understood profit and loss as well as any banker, and her keen business sense provided stability and even a few luxuries for her family in a time when such extras were hard to come by. What I learned from the example she set was and is beyond price, and although the money she made from selling eggs and frying chickens may not be considered much to crow about by many of today's standards, it certainly wasn't chicken feed.

CHAPTER 5

Decoration Day

To everything there is a season,
and a time to every purpose under the heaven.
—Ecclesiastes 3:1

%. %. %. %. %.

Three-day-weekend getaways, family barbecues, the Indy
500, and the unofficial beginning of summer. This is what
Memorial Day, the last Monday in May, evokes in the minds
of most people nowadays.

But when I was a child, Memorial Day was acknowledged
on May 30, the date designated for it in the proclamation
issued in 1868 by General John Logan, national commander
of the Grand Army of the Republic.

In fact, at our house we didn't even call the holiday
"Memorial Day"; for as long as I can remember it was always
called Decoration Day. There was nothing special about it for
us as far as holiday activities were concerned. Life went along
pretty much as usual: the men worked in the fields, cows were
milked morning and evening, livestock was fed, and eggs were
gathered from the chickens. Meals consisted of the standard

daily farm fare and were prepared and served as usual. For me, though, one of the special things that Decoration Day meant was that it marked the beginning of strawberry season and I could look forward to dining on shortcake every day for the next two weeks.

It was more than strawberry shortcake that really set the day aside, however, because this was the day that my mother and I gathered flowers and made a trip to decorate a dozen or so graves of relatives buried in two nearby Knox County cemeteries.

※ ※ ※ ※ ※

We had a certain ritual to our Decoration Day observances. Once the noon meal dishes were cleared — Mother washed while I dried and put away — Mother would get out her big butcher knife from the drawer and head outside to cut flowers from the flower beds that surrounded the house.

No special flower-clipping shears nor fancy flat-bottom baskets for the express purpose of gathering cut flowers were used by my mother. She didn't believe in such fripperies. Instead, she just stalked up to the unsuspecting peonies, irises, gladiolas, and dahlias and whacked away. If daisies or phlox were in bloom they also were subject to Mother's blade. A metal milk bucket filled with cool water to plunk the fresh-cut blossoms into accompanied her; when the gathering was done, she was ready to hit the road for our cemetery visits.

While Mother cut the flowers, I rummaged through the basement for the large-mouth glass canning jars that would serve as vases. We always had a fair supply of jars that had nicks around the top and weren't prime for canning anymore, and those were the ones I looked for. I brought them up in a couple of bushel baskets and dumped out whatever dead bugs might be nestled in the bottom. I didn't worry about cleaning them out any further; after all, once they got to the cemetery and were filled with flowers, there they stayed, never to be used again.

Our first stop was seven miles away, where Mother's family, the Bobes, were buried — her parents, aunts, uncles, sister, brother, and cousins. The Bobes were not in a family plot, so to visit each grave meant a meandering drive along the cemetery's winding roads until we located everyone. My job was to help her place the mixed bouquets into the glass jars and set them against the tombstones with the hope that they would survive for a few days; Mother could pretty much rest assured that the blossoms would still be at their peak freshness until her sisters arrived later in the day for their own cemetery deliveries, at which time they could nod their approval of Mother's fulfillment of her memorial mission.

After visiting the Bobe graves we made the almost-half-hour trip to the cemetery at the Upper Indiana Church — also called the "Brick Church" — in a rather secluded area in the countryside a bit north of Vincennes. (Aside from the cemetery visits, we seldom traveled this far north in the county, except to attend the church's annual picnic every August.) The McCormicks, my dad's family, were entombed there. Like the other cemetery, this one was very old, with some gravesites dating back a century or more, including that of my first McCormick relative, who arrived in Vincennes around 1800 (he lived to be in his sixties). Mother knew the exact location of each gravesite of the assorted McCormick relatives as well as she did those of her own family.

Mother went from grave to grave, arranging the flowers in the canning jars and setting them just so. If she was in a section that had several relatives together, she would let me wander among the gravestones, looking for those with familiar names. Some stones were so old the engraving was worn almost smooth from exposure to decades of weather. Several markers bore the names of young men who had died in the Civil War. For the most part, the names and information on the stones meant nothing to me. Still, the ground I walked on was hallowed, and I felt a sense of awe for the spirits of those who lay there.

My ancestors were not fallen war heroes. They were everyday people, farmers and their wives and children, whose lives simply had ended. But Mother's dedication to their memory was no less because of that.

These days, if you were to tell someone you had spent part of your holiday in a cemetery placing flowers at the graves of relatives, they would most likely think you had a few marbles missing. Why would anyone spend their time doing such a thing?

Tradition played a role, and of course family pressure — what would sisters and aunts and cousins think of Mother if she didn't make her visit? — but beyond that I believe she felt a sense of responsibility to the memory of these people, some gone so long that anyone who had known them was also long dead. They were family, and by honoring their memory a part of them was kept alive, and the family bonds strengthened. After all, knowing where and from whom we came is very much a part of who we are.

Mother always seemed somewhat matter-of-fact about the task, and I never saw her pause for prayer. The cost was minimal, a little time, a little gas, and some flowers from our own garden. Yet, at each cemetery, as we got in the car to head out, I gazed across the landscape and marveled at the deed. Where only lonely gray stones and grass had been, splashes of bright color decorated the scene. The beautiful flowers, whose heads bobbed gently in the late spring breeze, would be wilted and faded within a day or two. But for now, life had visited the cemeteries, and memories of long ago had been revived.

CHAPTER 6

Lessons Learned from Childhood Games

*I*t's next to impossible these days to pick up a newspaper or magazine without seeing at least one item on health problems of children brought on partly by overeating but primarily by inactivity.

When I was growing up, in the days before the onset of entertainment by television and computers, not getting enough exercise was definitely not a problem. When we weren't in school or doing our chores we were outdoors, playing. Whether it was in our own backyard, the sandlot at school, or in our classrooms during recess in inclement weather, we competed, cheated (don't tell!), and learned to get along with each other — sometimes on a "like it or not" basis.

Our games were active and sometimes rough and tumble: tag, hide and seek, Red Rover, and others. These were popular in the 1930s through the '50s; several have survived to this day as children's playtime classics. Some of them — unfortunately, I think — are no longer permitted on schoolyards for fear that a child may be injured (and parents might sue).

More than our bodies were exercised in these games, though; our minds also got a good workout organizing teams, planning strategies, and using principles of applied physics, as in games like jacks (bouncing balls) and jump-rope (velocity). And although we didn't realize it at the time, we were also gaining valuable life survival skills. We probably wouldn't have enjoyed the games so much if we'd thought we were learning something!

The bottom line was that we had fun. I sometimes think it would be great to be a kid again, and sometimes I ask myself, Why not be one, or at least act like one now and then? The only thing really different now from how I was sixty years ago is that I know my physical limits. My knees won't tolerate jumping rope, nor can I make a mad dash across a field to break through a Red Rover line; but I'll bet I could still scoop up a bunch of jacks on one bounce of the ball.

Now I can let my mind take me back in time. I can close my eyes and feel the exhilaration of making that dash across the field and the thrill of the air swooshing past my face as I go higher and higher on my backyard swing. The recollections alone are enough to get my heart pumping.

So let's walk down memory lane, rediscover what rules of the games there were, and find out what golden nuggets of wisdom we can glean.

TAG

I loved tag, especially on a Sunday afternoon when some of my cousins came over for dinner. Granted, there's no set rule as to how many could play, but this was the kind of game where "the more the merrier" definitely applied.

In tag, one player is designated "it" and the others scatter, keeping as far away from the pursuer as possible. When someone is tagged, he or she then becomes "it." Play continues until the recess bell rings, exhaustion sets in, or parents call the players home for supper.

Usually a kind of border or boundary is set, just to have some limits as to how far the players can run, which also gives "it" a better chance of tagging someone. Also included in the playing field are a couple of "bases," such as a tree trunk or a fencepost, where players can take a little respite from the game as long as they're touching "base."

Rules are few and far between, but a couple of common ones include "no tag back," which keeps a tagged player from immediately tagging the person who made them "it" right back. If nothing else, that at least gives the former "it" has a chance to catch his breath. "No tag backs" has to be claimed before the new "it" strikes, though.

Another tag no-no is "babysitting" base, a situation where "it" hovers so closely that the person on base is more or less trapped there and no one else can get on without risking immediately being tagged. Once "no babysitting" is said by a player, "it" should move away. Failure to comply with this rule can make "it" pretty unpopular for a while.

In many ways, life is a game of tag, where you may need to run like the dickens to stay ahead of the pack, all the while looking over your shoulder and dodging and evading being tagged. Agility and quick thinking can take you far. Also important is to make sure you have a "base" or two in life, a place of refuge you can escape to in order to catch your breath and think over life's situations.

As for whether being "it" is a good thing or a bad thing, I have mixed feelings. "It" does hold somewhat of a position of power, even if everyone else works hard to avoid you, not totally unlike some bosses. On the other hand, when you consider that you're "it" simply because you didn't run fast enough, maybe it's not such a great thing and you may want to do something about changing your position.

HIDE AND SEEK

*T*here's nothing like playing hide and seek on a farm in the early evening. The barn and other outbuildings along with more bushes than you could shake a stick at offer an abundance of hiding places, thus upping the excitement and the challenge.

Hide and seek is a variant of tag, with one person being "it" and the others trying to avoid her as much as possible. The main difference in this game, though, is that "it," also called the "seeker," covers her eyes while turning away from the players, often leaning against a tree or wall, and counts (usually) to ten in a manner to draw it out, such as "One one-hundred, two one-hundred, three one-hundred" and so on. While "it" is counting, the other players scatter and hide.

At the end of the count, the seeker calls out, "Ready or not, here I come!" and the hunt is on. As in tag, a "home base" is usually designated. If a player is found and can make it to home before the seeker does, that player is "safe" for the rest of the game as long as he stays there.

The point, of course, is to have the seeker find the hiders, or "outs," and the first one found who can't make it to home becomes "it." At this point, the new seeker calls out "Olly-olly-outs-in-free" (sometimes said "Olly-olly-oxen-free") to bring the other players in and restart the game — or call it off and move on to something else.

There are no real winners or losers in hide and seek, but the ones who can stay hidden the longest are considered the best players.

How many times have you wondered if you're hiding or seeking, if you're the hunted or the hunter? Knowing when to hide and when to seek may be the mark of a winner. Knowing when to blow your own horn or keep a low profile can go a long way in avoiding potential hassles. And sometimes, it's best to just play it safe and stick close to "home."

My older brothers were usually too busy to spend much time with me, so it was a real treat when my cousins — also my best girlfriends — came over to play. From left: Lois Marchino, Betty Marie Neal, Mary Marchino, and me.

RED ROVER

*T*here we stood on the school playground in two lines, holding hands, each line facing the other. Jimmy, the "captain" of the other team, had just called "Red Rover, Red Rover, let Strutsie come over!" I weighed my options carefully: Those were some pretty strong players over there, but Mary Ann tended to have a pretty weak grip, so I decided to go for that link. I took a deep breath and ran across the field for all I was worth, hoping I would break through ...

The game of Red Rover stayed popular clear into the 1970s, around which time our society became increasingly litigious and fear of the potential for players' injuries got it banned from most school and public playgrounds.

Granted, Red Rover can be a rough game. Two teams face each other, usually about twenty-five or thirty feet apart, and link hands to form lines. Whichever team gets first choice decides on a player from the other team and calls out, "Red Rover, Red Rover, let [player's name] come over!"

That player then has to run full tilt toward the other line with the goal of breaking through. If she doesn't, she has to join the team that called her. If she does, though, she gets to pick one of the two players whose link she broke and take that player with her back to her original team. The second team then calls "Red Rover" and the play continues back and forth until one of the teams has formed a super chain, at which point the game ends.

That recognition of hearing your name called, especially early in the game, is a heady experience. Hopefully, you're being acknowledged as both a good runner and a good team member. However, it may be that the team called on you because they think you're a weak player and can't break through. Well, then, just do your best to prove them wrong! If your name isn't called until the end, though, it's a good lesson in how to deal with rejection.

Either way, as we mature we learn that sometimes you have to break rank to achieve what you want, while at other times it's important to stay tight with the team you're on and not be the weak link. And if you end up on the side that's opposing your first one, learn to link hands with the ones there and be a good team player.

JUMP ROPE

W hen I was a youngster, rope jumping was strictly for girls; the only adults who jumped rope were boxers. It may not have been considered a competitive sport, but my girlfriends and I turned it into one, seeing who could outjump the others.

Nowadays we know that jumping rope is good exercise for everyone, male or female, child or adult, and few if any activities could be simpler: You hold a rope, one end in each hand, and swing it over your head and under your feet.

I always found jumping rope to be a lot more fun if I had a "counter," someone who would rhythmically chant the number of times I jumped before my feet disconnected from my brain and I got tangled in the rope. Better yet was having three to play, two twirling the rope as one jumped, or even, with a long-enough rope, having two spin while two jumped. That was way more challenging and took a whole lot more concentration.

Obviously, being fit and in good physical condition is a good thing for everyone, and jumping rope offers a cardiovascular workout not much different from jogging or bike riding. If you aren't jumping solo, though, teamwork offers healthy emotional and psychological benefits. Working together rather than as a lone player is considerably more enjoyable, but keep in mind that you need to coordinate your efforts and keep your balance in order to avoid tripping and getting tangled in the ropes and falling on your face.

TEETER-TOTTER

*M*y teeter-tottering was limited to school recesses and church picnics. Even if we'd had a teeter-totter at home, my older brothers Jim and Don were too busy to play with me, and little brother Eddie was too small (read, too lightweight) during the years he would have cared for it.

A companion is mandatory for teeter-tottering, no two ways about it. Two people sit facing each other on opposite ends of a board balanced in the middle by a cross-bar or other such support. Ideally the players are about the same weight, but the center point of the board can be adjusted sometimes if one outweighs the other. One player plants her feet on the ground and pushes off firmly but gently until her end is up in the air. The other player does the same; soon, momentum is established to keep a steady rhythm going. It's not exactly an exciting pastime, but it's relaxing and the face-to-face nature of it offers a chance to chat. Two more players can join in if the board is long enough. All in all, it's a relaxing way to kill time.

Marriage sometimes makes me think of teeter-totter. If there isn't much of a balance of power, there isn't much of a marriage. As long as you coordinate your efforts, things go along smoothly. If one ends

*up being the "heavy," though, he or she may decide
to hold their own end of the board down and leave
their partner high and dry up in the air with no
footing on solid ground. On the other hand, if the
one holding the board down decides he has had
enough and just hops off abruptly, his partner on
the other side comes crashing down on her rear end
— HARD!*

SWINGING

*A*n enormous old maple tree stood in our yard just outside the dining room window, and a swing hung by ropes from its lowest branch. That branch wasn't so low, however, that you couldn't get really good loft in the swing, and there was nothing to compare to seeing if I could go high enough for my toes to brush the tree's leaves.

Swinging is about the most straightforward play activity there is. You sit on a seat suspended by ropes or chains and swing; you get yourself started with a little push-off with your feet, then pump your legs rhythmically back and forth and lean into the momentum, going ever higher and higher. It's as close to flying as you can get without leaving the ground, and one of the most exhilarating activities I've ever done. It's an acquired skill, though, and very small children usually need an adult or older child to push them until they get the hang of how to swing by themselves.

There was nothing quite like my first swing there in our side yard on the farm. The limb was high and the ropes were long, so if I pumped hard enough I could soar really high. For a little extra challenge and excitement, when I got as high as I could go, I'd spring

from the seat and fly through the air and land squarely
— I hoped! — on my feet.

%% %% %% %% %%

*When we first start out on an endeavor, we may
need someone to push us gently but firmly until we
get going. Once we get the hang of it, however, we
learn that if we really work at it we can really soar.
We may still need a little push now and then, but
that's okay. We can't do everything by ourselves!*

JACKS

I loved playing jacks, but it was a game saved more or less for times when the weather didn't permit running around outdoors at school during recess. It could really bring out the killer instinct sometimes: There was nothing like a half-dozen eight-year-olds competing at jacks to get things livened up!

Jacks may be one of the ultimate games to develop a child's hand-eye coordination. Fifteen jacks, small metal six-pointed star-like objects, are scattered loosely onto a flat surface. The first player calls how many jacks she plans to pick up, starting out usually with "onesies," "twosies," and so on. She then bounces a small rubber ball on the surface and, with the same hand, scoops up the jacks, catching the ball before it bounces again. The ultimate challenge is to grab all the jacks and the ball in one sweep without dropping any of them, a tricky feat achieved by only the most dexterous.

Life is a juggling process, and often we feel like we have too many balls in the air. Concentrating on keeping just one ball in play at a time may be the best course, but you need to really keep a sharp eye

on both that and whatever else you're reaching for. Grabbing opportunities can be a lot like grabbing jacks: keep adding as you go through life, scoop up as many as you can, but try not to fumble them.

PICK-UP STICKS

*P*ick-up sticks was a game for us kids to play whenever we couldn't go outside for some reason. It was a quiet game that could keep us occupied and out from under-foot for a long time, something any adult would appreciate.

Pick-up sticks is a two-player game consisting of long, thin sticks in various colors, with each color worth different numbers of points. One player holds the bundle of sticks with the bottoms resting on a flat surface. The sticks are let go, after which each player takes a turn to pull one out without disturbing the rest of the pile, sometimes by using a helper stick. If any stick other than the one selected moves, the turn is over. This game requires considerable concentration and dexterity, and it can be frustrating — but you have to learn to deal with that.

What does this say about life? When you're picking something or someone to remove from a group, you should take care that the rest of the group doesn't end up in total disarray, and that it can continue to function. While it's true that no one is truly indispensable, if the group falls apart because of your selection, you probably will have to start over from scratch.

A bunch of classmates (first and second grades here) and a beautiful day — perfect for a game of tag or Red Rover. I'm in the top row, second from left.

STRING FIGURES

A summer day, a tree to lean against, and a loop of string around my fingers. Aside from lying on my back looking for animal shapes in the clouds, I couldn't imagine a better way to pass some lazy time when I was a kid.

Jacob's ladder, cat's cradle — these are only a couple of string figures that have been popular for centuries. Making a string figure involves a loop of string held around the fingers of both hands and moving the fingers in such ways as to form a design. The real fun begins as more and more complex configurations are attempted while trying to not get your hands tied up in knots or drop a loop.

Sometimes we're able to weave beautiful patterns in our lives with just a few twists and turns. If you don't pay attention, though, you may find it's hard to completely avoid getting knotted up, which can cause all kinds of difficulty. Play the game right and concentrate on what you're doing and you'll usually not only accomplish your goal, but feel good about it too.

MUSICAL CHAIRS

I played this several times when I was a young child and enjoyed it somewhat, but after awhile being bumped on my bottom onto the floor lost its appeal. By the time I was a mature twelve years old, my friends and I had moved onto other party games.

A time-honored game at young children's birthday parties, musical chairs involves a number of players who move around a group of chairs arranged in a circle and facing outward, with one chair fewer than there are players. Music is played, during which the participants walk around the chairs. When the music stops, everyone races to sit down. Whoever is left without a chair is out, and that sometimes leads to a lot of pushing and shoving, ending up with someone on the floor. The chairless person is sent to the side, another chair is removed, and the game resumes until only one player is left.

If you like moving around in circles and being shoved and shuffled, mindlessly waiting for the music to stop, then this is the game for you.

CHAPTER 7

August

*S*ummertime has long been celebrated in song, with Nat "King" Cole extolling the "lazy, hazy days" and the Gershwin brothers waxing poetic on how "the livin' is easy."

Not on our farm. The days may have been hazy, but they certainly were never lazy, nor was the livin' easy. Summer was the busy season because along with the year-round duties of caring for livestock there was planting and crop-tending to be done, and workdays lasted literally from sunup to sundown. The men spent long hours in the fields, sometimes not even able to take time out to come home to eat at noon, and the women would have to deliver the meal to them. Meantime, the women worked in the vegetable gardens that would feed their families not only during the summer months but also during the winter, which involved hours spent canning the produce for safekeeping, as well as the daily chore of preparing the big midday meals for all the hands in the fields, milking the cows, and gathering the eggs.

Our farm, like all others, was of course a family business and everyone in the family had to pitch in and do their share. As young children, my brothers' and my chores were simple, such as helping with the garden and fetching and delivering, but we were expected to meet our responsibilities with no questions asked. As we got older our workload increased, with the boys having outdoor work with crops and livestock. As the only girl, I never had to work in the fields or do any of the really heavy labor and my mother spared me the task of ever having to milk the cows. "I milked enough cows when I was a girl to cover for both of us," she told me (her family had owned a dairy). Still, I had plenty on my plate, being Mother's assistant with all of the rest of her work and I certainly never had the complaint of "nothing to do."

Nonetheless, with all that kept us occupied in the summers on the farm, after awhile we missed our school friends and longed for the school routine. Due to the farm planting schedules, the summer school break in rural areas lasted from mid-April until after Labor Day. That was a long time to go without the daily socializing my classes and friends provided. We saw some friends and family at church on Sundays, and I remember listening with envy as some of the older kids stood outside after services and made plans to go to the movie in town that evening. Oh, to be a teenager!

My true summer salvation came when I turned nine and joined 4-H and had weekly club meetings to look forward to, and as I grew older and became more proficient in my skills learned in 4-H, I had something else to really look forward to: August, the month for both the county and state fairs where my brothers and I would submit our summer projects — livestock for them, baking, food preparation and presentation, and sewing for me — and it was a thrill to see how many ribbons and awards we could bring home.

August was also the month in which some of the churches in Knox County held their annual picnics. By that

Extension Bulletin No. 264   May, 1941

4-H CLUB BAKING

First Division
(To Be Used for Project Work Only)

Collect your small utensils on a tray and you will have them handy;
you will also save time.

"LET'S MAKE A CAKE"

Cooperative Extension Work in Agriculture and Home Economics
State of Indiana, Purdue University
and the United States Department of Agriculture Cooperating
H. J. Reed, Director, Lafayette, Indiana
Issued in furtherance of the Acts of May 8 and June 30, 1914.

My first 4-H Club Baking booklet.

65

time all of the crops were more or less in a holding pattern, just putting in their time ripening until the fall harvest, so even the men's schedules were less busy, and everyone in our little community was ready for a good time, looking forward to catching up with friends and neighbors we'd seen little of during the busy months, and relaxing and enjoying the fruits of the summer's labors.

※ ※ ※ ※ ※

The church picnics started early in the month, one every week so each could have its turn. These were ecumenical affairs, come-one-come-all, regardless of what affiliation you might have, and come all they did, folks from all around the area, including regulars from nearby Vincennes (whom we referred to as the "town people").

Our little church, Trinity Methodist, held their event on the first Thursday in August (the first in the season) and it was a big deal in the life of not only this country girl, but everyone involved. These picnics were a labor of love and the essence of volunteerism, but all in all, they were indeed a labor. The affair itself started at five on the designated afternoon, but the getting-ready activity began several days before, what with the planning and the signing-up of who would do and/or bring what.

Tasks and contributions were settled, and on the morning of the picnic, those who had volunteered to help set up gathered on the church's lawn and put up the tables, chairs, and various activity-booth structures that would be needed.

Dawn of the big day found the church women, Mother included, scurrying around their kitchens preparing whatever foods they had signed up to provide. Mother volunteered to do much more than I can remember, but I do know that there was nothing fancy-schmancy about the food she contributed to the picnic — hearty country fare comprised the menu. By mid-afternoon it was time to pack up and get ready to go.

The ready-to-eat food brought by the volunteers like my mother was set up as close as possible to the picnic start time so everything would be fresh, and when the folks got in line to load up their plates, it was indeed a sight to behold. There it was: long cafeteria-style tables laden with fried chicken, ham, baked beans, potato salad, cole slaw, green beans, cucumbers, pickles, sliced tomatoes, rolls and breads, and a mind-boggling selection of desserts. Lemonade and iced tea were available at the end of the food service line, or diners could opt for a soft drink from the pop stand. An ice cream stand with a stocked freezer provided by the local creamery offered a creamy treat to top home-baked pies and cobblers.

Everyone in our small congregation knew who fixed what and looked forward to the sampling. Unfortunately, the workers were the last to eat, so sometimes their favorites were gone before they got to the table.

As far as I was concerned, though, the culinary highlight of the day was the church's famous fricassee, a thick stew more or less indigenous to the southern-Indiana region that contained chicken, bacon, ground beef, onions, barley, and beans, all in a tomato-juice-based broth. The ingredients were gathered at the picnic site early in the day to allow for the long cooking process the dish involved, simmering for hours in an enormous black cast-iron caldron located outside the back door of the church. On paper the fricassee (also known as a "burgoo") may not sound so good, but it was an absolute delicacy, one we had only in August, and the gallons and gallons of it were made because it was so popular that people (especially the townspeople) not only ate their fill of it at the picnic, they also often brought containers to take some home to freeze for later dining. Each church had its own closely guarded recipe for fricassee and it was always a challenge to determine whose was best. Of course, we were sure *ours* was!

Different groups in the church had fundraising projects from ring toss games to grab bags. When I was a teenager, our youth group (all ten of us) claimed the fish pond that consisted of a tarpaulin wrapped around a tree, making a small structure for one person working inside. The game player would swing a fishing-pole line over the top and the worker inside would attach a trinket, purchased from a wholesaler, onto the end. The teens' profits for the evening usually totaled about twenty dollars, the proceeds going into the treasury of the Methodist Youth Fellowship.

Trinity's picnics didn't last far into the evening. The next day was an early morning work day for farm folks, so by around eight chairs were being folded and tables cleaned to have everything in order for the set-up crew to break down and cart away. By nine P.M. everyone was on their way home. By noon Friday — the following day — you couldn't tell there had been a picnic on the church grounds. Even the sparse grass (there were too many trees to have thick grass) was barely dented from all of the cars that had parked on it.

St. Peter's Lutheran Church on Old Decker Road held their picnic on the third Thursday in August. Things there were pretty much the same except their teen group had no fish pond, their fricassee was of course slightly different, and the crowd was probably more Lutheran than Methodist, with many of our Catholic neighbors there too. In my teen years I really looked forward to St. Peter's picnics because that's where my boyfriend attended church and I always got to see him there.

The fourth Thursday's was claimed by the Upper Indiana Presbyterian Church for their picnic. The church was somewhat north of Vincennes; we called it "The Brick" and my McCormick family ancestors were buried in its cemetery. Same menu but naturally a slightly different crowd, more Presbyterians and folks from further north in Knox County.

The Catholics of St. Vincent's Church just outside Vincennes and St. Thomas' Church in our township were what we staid Protestants considered the "racy" group. Their picnics were held on church-owned grounds near the church, and were a lot different from the others, always held on Sunday and always included — gasp! — gambling! They started early, just before noon, and their revelry lasted until much later in the evening than the other churches' did. As I recall, they also offered — another gasp! — beer for sale. How decadent we thought those people were.

※ ※ ※ ※ ※

Despite the social whirl of the picnics, because school had been out since mid-April I was looking forward to its start the day after Labor Day. Through the long summer season the only breaks I had in my work routine were connected with 4-H, working on my projects, and attending club meetings. Most fun was the annual three-day camp at Shakamak State Park for 4-H kids.

All 4-H projects had to be completed by the time of the township exhibition in July. Our work was judged in the competition there, and winning a blue ribbon (first prize) made you eligible to send your project to the county fair in August. Baked goods, of course, were perishable and had to be reproduced for the county fair, and the State Fair also, if you were lucky enough to get that far. I always held my breath that mine would turn out right for each competition.

In the days I participated in 4-H, projects were clearly defined by gender: Boys competed in livestock, and girls competed in home and family arts like baking and sewing. Sometimes a girl had livestock, such as a calf, sheep, or hog, but frankly, I wasn't interested in that. I got my fill of tending animals just by looking after our chickens every day. Besides, showing livestock, as my brothers did, involved having to stay overnight with them at the fairgrounds because they had to be fed, watered, and groomed. *That* certainly was not for me!

I enjoyed baking (I still do, more so than any other type of cooking) and submitted cakes for competition every year, even taking the Grand Champion — with its big purple ribbon! — at the State Fair one year for my Pineapple Upside-Down Cake. Sewing, though, was my true passion. Over the years my projects graduated from boring little tea towels to a full clothing ensemble, for which I got my very first pair of high-heeled pumps. The love of sewing never left me and I continued to make almost all of my own clothes into my fifties.

I went to the fairs only when I had something special to do, such as model my sewing project in the dress revue. Our family, like most, had only one car, so Mother hauled us the fourteen miles until I turned sixteen and got my driver's license. After that, she stayed home and let me take care of those treks. She knew she didn't have to worry about us getting into mischief. Farm life is a well-disciplined one, and farm kids tended to be well behaved. We never even considered doing anything outside the "boundaries." We might stroll

Eddie's calf, his 4-H project, didn't mind standing still for a good brush-down.

through the midway and go on an occasional ride, but for the most part we looked upon the carnival operations with a degree of suspicion. The carnies seemed to be a wild bunch compared to the folks we knew, so beyond the few rides and games we played we kept our distance. Besides, the sights I was interested in seeing didn't involve the midway itself. I rarely saw any of boys from my school because most of them weren't in 4-H, but a lot of the ones from farther around the county were well worth looking at!

Once the county fair was over, most 4-H'ers who had been awarded Grand Champion on their projects sent those along to the Indiana State Fair in Indianapolis. Attending that was a really special event for me; I didn't get to go until I was a teen-ager because the distance, 125 miles, made it prohibitive unless I was participating in something.

Without a doubt, though, the biggest thrill of my young life was when I participated in the Indiana State Fair Girls' School in the summer before my last year of high school. Located on the State Fairgrounds in a 4-H dormitory, the school was a ten-day educational event, and only one girl from each of Indiana's ninety-two counties was selected, so it really was quite an honor. Mornings were spent in 4-H-related classes and afternoons involved attending every competitive event that took place during the fair. We always had a designated seating section for these events, and we were easy to spot in the crisp uniforms we were required to wear whenever we were on the fairgrounds in a group.

It was so much fun to meet girls from all over the state. We were broken down into small groups of a dozen or so headed by Honor Girls, young women who had just graduated from high school who served as "mother hens," helping us with problems or giving us information about our activities. The

Honor Girls were chosen by the Fair School's staff based on their class achievements and leadership abilities. As delighted as I was to attend the school in the first place, imagine my surprise when I was selected as one of these special people.

My Honor Girl year was especially exciting, and highlighted by my dad's being a special guest at the fair. He was President Truman's Undersecretary of Agriculture and spent most of his time in Washington, D.C., and I was tickled to be able to spend some extra time with him during that week.

%% %% %% %% %%

The State Fair was over and the 4-H'ers relaxed and basked in our blue-ribbon glory (or not). Thoughts of projects and competitions faded away until the next May when it started all over again. Those who had won awards could look forward to seeing their names listed in their local newspapers. That's about all of the gratification there was in 4-H: no money (unless you sold your livestock), just pats on the back. There was a sense of purity to the system.

Touches of brown and gold in the trees, gusty winds stirring up little dust spirals, and an occasional chilly, breezy night told us that August was over also. The church picnics, except for the St. Vincent's on Labor Day weekend, were history until the next year.

I had graduated high school and 4-H would now be just a memory. My days now were spent preparing for a new adventure, starting college at Purdue University. I was packed and ready to go — a clock radio, an Underwood portable typewriter, and my clothes. My suitcase wasn't that big, and the dorm rooms were small, so I had to take care and pack as efficiently as possible.

The most precious things I took with me required no space in my suitcase, for they were safely packed in my mind. I took memories of August, 4-H, the fairs, and picnics. But these memories went beyond the good times. I had learned about teamwork and cooperation; I had learned how to handle winning and losing; I had learned about doing your best for its sake alone. And packed in my heart were the friendship and love that came with all of these August things.

CHAPTER 8

Going to Town

"**S**trutsie!" my mother called as she looked for me. "Strutsie, where are you! Come on now, I'm ready — " Her words cut off sharply before I had a chance to answer her, and she couldn't help but smile. It was Saturday, her weekly going-to-town day, and at age seven I was going with her for the first time. I had no intention of holding things up, so there I was, already in the front seat of our trusty Dodge, ready to go.

I remember that morning in early June 1942 so clearly. The day before, as Mother prepared her list of things she needed to get, I moped around watching her. "I wish I could go shopping tomorrow with you," I sighed, and couldn't believe my ears when she said, "Well, if you get up early and get your chores done, I don't see why not."

My two older brothers never got to go on these excursions (with good reason, though, because of all the work they had to do around the farm on weekends) and little brother Eddie, at five years of age, was too much of a handful to keep an eye on and get errands done too. This was really a big event for me because Vincennes, the Knox County seat, was all of seven miles away, almost in another world as far as I was concerned, and in those World War II days of single-car families and gas rationing, trips that far weren't made more than once a week at most.

The trunk of the car had already been loaded with several cases of eggs to take to the hatchery, each one holding fifteen dozen, plus a couple dozen extra in "special" egg baskets to deliver to friends in Vincennes. I was fidgety, eager to get started, but had to wait until Mother finished taking the Sunday cake out of the oven and placing it on a rack to cool while we were gone. Hoping to make the waiting go faster I grabbed the broom and swept the back porch. Finally, I could see that Mother was almost finished, so I changed into a school dress — one did not dress "casually" when going to town! — and while Mother changed her dress, put on her hat, and gathered her pocketbook, banking needs, shopping list, and car keys, I hopped into the car. You know the rest.

We pulled out of the driveway and onto Hart Street Road, which ran perpendicular to our front yard and ended there. Many a stranger came down that gravel road only to find themselves in a quandary: clearly they couldn't go straight on, and it wasn't unusual to have them knock at our front door, wondering if they were on the right direction to their destination. Rural roads had the tendency to be confusing (and still do, actually), full of turns, dead-ends, and T intersections like the one in front of our home. More often than not the strangers were woefully off the mark, and even after giving them meticulous directions, they would probably need to stop again at another farm house to ask the way.

"Well, Strutsie," Mother said after we had driven for a while — she always called me by my nickname unless she was peeved with me over something — "you certainly have been a good girl today. Why don't you help me steer the car

Mother's ready at the wheel, and we're going to town!

77

for a bit?" Well, I didn't have to be asked twice. I scooted across the big bench seat and put my hands on the steering wheel. This was only the second time I had been allowed to do this, and I could feel my face flush with pleasure. I felt so grown up!

At last we were on Hart Street and heading into town. The first stop was the hatchery, where one of the men helped Mother unload the eggs and tallied up her account. She tucked the money from the egg sale into her purse and we drove a bit farther on to Main Street, found a convenient parking space, and went into the American National Bank on the corner of Third and Main so Mother could get her banking done before they closed at noon.

Finished with the banking business, we went back out onto Main Street and walked along the shopping district. There were so many stores with so much to see, and Mother indulged me and allowed me to take my time to gawk a bit. I had never seen such things, like the glittering jewelry arrayed in Simon's window, or the fine suits in Albert's Men's Store. Pair after pair of shoes were displayed at Johnson's Bootery, and the lovely dresses in the window of La Rose, the ladies' clothing store, dazzled me. My mother had always made all of her clothes and mine, so I was amazed that there was such a thing as ready-to-wear.

My mouth watered when we passed by and saw the shelves in Greek's Candy Store laden with more candy than I had ever seen in one place. We stopped at the Montgomery Ward and J. C. Penney department stores, and the dime stores, Kresge's and Woolworth's. It all was heaven to me, and as far as I was concerned, Vincennes' Main Street was paved with gold.

By this time it was close to noon. "I could use a bite to eat," Mother said. "How about you?" Of course I was hungry — I was a growing child and almost always hungry — but I was puzzled. Did Mother have some sandwiches in her pocketbook? Imagine my surprise when we went into Gimbel Bond, another department store, and sat down at their lunch counter. The closest I had ever come to "eating out" was either at a relative's home or at a church picnic. Mother ordered a chicken salad sandwich for us to share, and a glass of milk for me and iced tea for herself. She let me have the pickle that came with the sandwich, and although it really wasn't nearly as good as the pickles Mother made, I thought it was the best one I'd ever eaten.

Full and happy, we went back to the car and drove to the home of Agnes Barnes, a regular stop for Mother, to deliver one of the baskets of eggs. Miss Barnes was an elderly spinster lady whose parents built the house we lived in and from whom we bought that and a hundred acres of land. She was glad to see Mother and we sat in her parlor to visit and catch up on the news from the previous week. Miss Barnes was a sweet lady.

"What do I owe you for the eggs, Emma?" Miss Barnes asked as we got ready to leave.

"Now, Miss Barnes," Mother said, patting her hand. "You know I wouldn't take a cent from you. I'm glad to bring them to you."

They went back and forth for a moment or two. Mother was as insistent on *not* taking Miss Barnes' money as Miss Barnes was on wanting to pay, and Mother always prevailed. (This happened every week, Mother told me.) It was a good lesson to see how to be kind and charitable to someone and still preserve the person's dignity.

We made a couple more stops to deliver the second egg basket to some other family acquaintances, and Mother did accept payment for those. (In time, Mother would have me figure out how much they owed us. That was how I learned to do numbers in my head, something I have never forgotten.)

Before we left town we went to the A&P grocery for a few staples like flour, sugar, and salt, and finally to the frozen-food locker to pick up whatever meat we would need for the coming week. The meat was from our own animals that were butchered, but in those days before deep freezers were common home appliances, farm families rented storage space at these lockers.

I studied the street names as we drove through town. Even though I was just a beginning reader, I could make out a few of them, especially those short ones with names of trees like Elm and Oak, or Hart and Main, the ones most traveled. I wondered how Mother kept from getting lost.

It had been a long day, so I climbed into the back seat so I could lie down and rest awhile. The next thing I knew the car was crunching on our gravel driveway, and we were home.

%. %. %. %. %.

Over the years I took many more trips to town with Mother. I didn't get to go every week, and it was more special because of that. We didn't always get lunch, but often we would go into Smith's Drugstore and share a soda at their fountain on our way home. I enjoyed our visits to Gimbel Bond's yard goods section because then I could help select fabrics and trim for whatever new frocks Mother was planning for me. Occasionally I could wheedle her into buying me a small treat at Greek's or from one of the dime stores. "Don't tell your brothers," she warned me each time. Of course, I could hardly wait to get home and tell! Maybe that was one reason they called me "The Princess."

I turned sixteen and got my driver's license and was now and then allowed to take the car and drive into Vincennes myself. It took some doing to learn my way around because when the French first settled and platted the town in the early 1700s, they did it in the French way and logic was not a primary consideration. The streets ran east from the Wabash River and bent here and there in a rather haphazard fashion, and it was never clear whether you were headed east, west, north, or south. The confusion was exacerbated by some of the main streets continuing out into the countryside: Main Street Road, Hart Street Road, and Old Decker Road. (Even trickier, the road that T'd at our house was *Lower* Hart Street Road, as opposed to *Upper* Hart Street Road.) Anyone who visited from a place where streets ran parallel and perpendicular just about pulled their hair out.

I never could get navigating the streets totally straight in my head and still can't, but the street names are delightful. Vincennes has twenty-seven of them named for trees, ranging alphabetically from Ash to Willow. The next most popular name category is places, nine in all including Chicago, Indianapolis, and Minneapolis. American presidents are honored: Lincoln, Harrison, Jackson, Jefferson, Washington, and in mid-1960s, Kennedy. Grouseland Drive is named for President William Henry Harrison's home where he lived when he was governor of the Indiana Territory (and which is still a popular tourist destination). Monticello Drive is dubbed after Thomas Jefferson's home in Virginia.

A French flavor can be found in street names like Dubois, Busseron, Rousillion, Lafayette, and Guerretaz Forest. The native Americans who lived in the area and elsewhere around the nation have not been ignored, and many street signs bear such names as Seminole, Delaware, and Cherokee.

Chief Tecumseh, the Shawnee leader who went head-to-head with William Henry Harrison, got his due also. A couple of American heroes, Vigo and Clark, are acknowledged, and names like Bayou, Wabash, and Deer Path Trail evoke the town's rustic past. (My favorites, because they are so unusual, are Coal Chute Road and Ft. Knox Place.)

Much of what I was familiar with in Vincennes as I was growing up is gone. Main Street still runs through the town's heart, and the population, about twenty thousand, is pretty much the same; but none of the stores of my childhood are there, all of them having been replaced with less-important shops that don't represent the life I remember.

Nowadays, when I go to Vincennes to visit family, I get off at the Hart Street exit from the Highway 50 bypass. Clustered there are a Starbucks, a K-Mart, and other chain and big-box stores. If I need to get some cash, one of the modern banks in the area has a drive-through ATM. I have no need to go downtown. Perhaps it's just as well. In my memories I can still look in the shop windows, stroke the fabrics in Gimbel Bond's, and taste the chocolate soda at Smith's.

Some things never change though. Vincennes will always boast the George Rogers Clark Memorial, St. Francis Xavier Catholic Church (better known as the Old Cathedral), which is the oldest established church in the Northwest Territory, the Lincoln Frieze on the Illinois side of the bridge over the Wabash River, Vincennes University, and the twenty-seven streets named for trees. Vincennes will always be able to claim Red Skelton as its own native son and its surrounding area will always produce the best cantaloupes and watermelons in the state (if not the country).

Vincennes will always hold a special place in my heart. It was there that I fashioned my ideas on shopping, banking, time organization, and efficiency. Most important, Vincennes was where I spent special Saturday afternoons with my mother and learned the value of going to town.

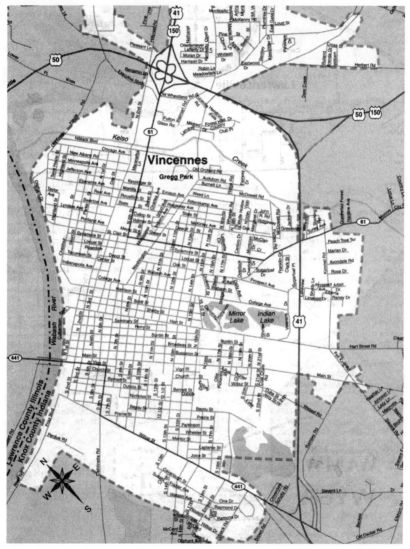

Names of trees, names of presidents, and names of Indians, spiced up with a few with a decidedly French flavor — those are the streets of Vincennes.

CHAPTER 9

1941
Holidays and Storm Clouds

November 20, 1941

t was still early. The gray light of the late autumn morning filtered in around the curtains and the wind rattled the windows as if it wanted to come in and play. I burrowed down under the blanket, enjoying the toasty warmth and wanting to stay in bed for a while longer, but the teasing wind lured me from my cozy lair.

I tossed off the covers and stretched, rubbing the sleep from my eyes. Faintly, I could hear activity from the kitchen; my nose twitched and detected not as faintly the usual breakfast aromas — but there was something else.

Turkey! I climbed out of bed and scurried over to the register where the warm air rising from the coal furnace in the basement billowed around my legs. I pushed the curtain aside and looked outside. By this time of year the trees and shrubs were bare, and what leaves hadn't already been blown away scudded around the yard like confetti. The swing that hung from the low limb of the big maple swayed back and forth in the wind, inviting me to come out and sit awhile, despite the chill.

I felt a soft movement at my elbow and looked down to see my little brother, Eddie, at my side. "Strutsie, d'you think Mother will let us go out and play?" he asked, still sleepy-eyed. I hugged him. "If we're good and do our chores, I hope she will," I said. At age five, he was only eighteen months younger than I, but still looked up to me as a figure of authority, a position I relished.

I sent him back to his room to get dressed while I pulled my own clothes on, and we both tumbled into the kitchen. Eddie and I sat down to steaming bowls of CoCo Wheats ("the creamy hot cereal with the cocoa treat") and watched Mother bustle around while we ate. A pile of cubed bread, seasonings, and celery sat to one side of the kitchen sink, ready to be combined for the dressing she would make later, and now she was busy mixing her famous rich date pudding to take to Grandma and Grandpa McCormick's for Thanksgiving dinner as she always did. Many others of our family who would be there would bring lots of food also, but for hearty farm appetites, there was no such thing as "too much."

"Hurry and finish there so you can help me get things cleared away before your father and the boys get back from chores," Mother admonished us. They had risen long before dawn to get their morning chores done earlier than usual and would be heading over to Grandpa's farm to join a group of uncles and cousins for their traditional Thanksgiving hunt. I had watched Dad the night before as he fetched the shotgun and rifle from the back of his closet that was located just off the dining room. He checked his ammunition supply, after which my twelve-year-old brother Don, with Eddie's help, lined the shotgun shells up along the edge of the kitchen table like little soldiers. Dad indulged their game for a bit, then collected the shells and stuffed enough for the day into the pockets of his hunting jacket.

Eddie mushed around in his CoCo Wheats and grumbled, "I want to go hunting too." I felt a pang; ever since he was big enough to toddle, this little brother had been my constant playmate, my best buddy. Before too long I knew he would outgrow playing girl games with me and go off to the more manly pastimes of our older siblings. I still had a few years left before he would be old enough for those, though, and took comfort in that.

My oldest brother Jim, seventeen, was a veteran of the annual excursion and used the rifle while Dad toted the heavier and more unwieldy shotgun. My other brother Don, at age eleven, was experiencing his first year out with the men. Even though he was still relegated to using just his trusty BB gun until he was older he was excited to be included in the group, regardless of the early hour and the cold. Don was actually the biggest hunting fanatic of the family, heading out regularly on expeditions even when he was just a "little feller." The biggest game he bagged for the most part, though, was a handful of cookies from Harriet Kirk's kitchen just down the road.

Eddie and I finished our breakfast and I rinsed out the bowls and set them at the side of the sink. Then it was into sweaters, coats, caps, and mittens. Meantime, Dad and my older brothers had come back from chores, changed into their hunting garb, collected their gear, and headed out. We filed out the back door together, Eddie and I to play our games of leaf chasing, tag, and swinging and the "big guys" to bag their own game. We all would catch up with each other later at Grandpa's.

Eddie and I were tough farm kids, but the nip in the air and the sharp gusts of wind brought us back indoors after only a couple of hours. By then Mother had finished with her food preparations and it was time to clean up, change clothes, and get ready to go. We helped carry the food out and stash it securely in the trunk of the car, and with my little brother and I in the back seat and Mother driving, we made the five-mile trip to Grandma and Grandpa's. It was such a short trip that the food was still hot when we got there and didn't need any reheating, a good thing because since so much food was brought by everyone, it couldn't have possibly fit into Grandma's cook-stove oven.

Mother and Grandma and the aunts contributed different items to the meal: pies, cakes, puddings, and side dishes such as dressings — a couple with oysters, a special holiday treat — and others without. Turkeys were never stuffed because while several in the family favored the oyster dressing, not everyone else cared for it. I wasn't too crazy about it myself; on a couple of occasions I had watched Mother pick through the glistening, gray bits of seafood to make sure no clinging shell bits remained, and it looked like a slimy and unappetizing job to my untrained eye.

The turkey we brought was companion to the one Grandma had roasted, thus ensuring there would be enough for everybody at dinner and for leftovers. Rounding out the holiday menu would be homemade chicken and noodles, sauerkraut and wieners, and home-canned vegetables. The shortage of fresh vegetables available in late autumn didn't bother me at all; I was glad because I wanted to stuff myself on the "real" food, especially Aunt Dorothy's Parker House rolls, also a special treat because Mother never made them at home. Dad would tease me, saying, "Would you like a roll with your butter, Lorene?" as I poked the sweet, creamy stuff into the fold of my roll until it squished out the sides.

As we pulled up in front of Grandpa's house we saw that Aunt Dorothy (one of Dad's sisters) and Uncle Eph, who lived near Fritchton, had already arrived with their three children in tow. Several of our cousins went to the same church we did — Trinity Methodist — and we saw them every week, but we were eager to see and play with these cousins because they attended Old Cathedral Catholic Church in Vincennes and we didn't get to spend time with them very often. Cousin Maurice was close to Don's age; Mary was six, a year younger than I; and Lois was just a tad behind Eddie, so everyone had a playmate.

We had barely had time to hang up our coats before Aunt Midah, another of Dad's sisters, came bustling in with her husband Clarence and their six children. They lived nearby and we saw them every Sunday, but still Aunt Midah's younger children, Marion and Betty Marie, were also close enough to our ages to add to the playtime fun; Gladys, Ed, Alfred, and Dorothy Mae were old enough that my oldest brother Jim had someone more "grown up" to spend time with.

The hunters, meantime, had been back for some while and were busy dressing their day's take on Grandpa's back porch. It had been a good hunt and their bags were stuffed with rabbits and quail. At least some of those would be cooked over the weekend, and oh, how we looked forward to that once-a-year treat! Even with the aroma of turkey, dressing, and all the Thanksgiving accompaniments hanging in the air, just the thought of the tasty game fried in drippings until crispy on the outside and oh-so juicy on the inside made my mouth water.

The house seemed full to bursting by then, but we found out it had plenty enough room for more when Dad's younger brother John, along with his wife Lucy and their children, Wanda and Bill, came through the door bearing another pie and some green beans.

"Are Earl's going to make it?" Uncle John asked about the brother from Indianapolis. No, he was told, not this year.

Maybe it was just as well that Uncle Earl and his family had made other plans. Where in the world would Grandma have put them?

While dinner preparations were finished up, we children had to find something to do. It was too cold to play outside (plus, our mothers didn't want us getting dirty), and because the house didn't have central heat, the upstairs rooms weren't much better, so we had to make do by playing in the sitting room and being on our best behavior. Grandpa's leather daybed occupied one corner of the room; he spent a good part of his afternoons there taking a nap, using his unfolded newspaper as a cover so just his head and feet stuck out. An overstuffed chair, where he sat when he wanted to actually *read* the paper, occupied a place near the front door and was accompanied by a side table that held the radio and Grandpa's cigar supplies. He loved his cigars, and we kids loved the smell of them that lingered in the room because, for us, that was part of Grandpa.

Grandma's chair was centered in the room between Grandpa's and the bedroom, an indication perhaps of who truly was the center of the family.

At last dinner was ready and we were called to the table. The adults and older kids took their places at the big round table in the dining room and we of the younger set were sent to eat at the oilcloth-covered table in the kitchen. We really didn't mind because we found grown-up conversation boring anyway, and in the kitchen we didn't have to mind our manners so carefully.

About halfway through dinner the talk in the dining room became quiet, an automatic signal for those of us in the kitchen to prick up our ears and listen. After all, when adults talked very quietly it usually was because they didn't want the kids to hear.

"Things in Europe don't look like they're gonna get any better, do they?" Uncle Eph said. "Seems like that Hitler wants to take over every country there."

"It's pretty serious," my dad agreed. "It's bound to affect the economy in this country before too long, what with the blockades and all. Who knows what it might do to crop prices." Dad, who worked for the Indiana State Committee of the Agricultural Adjustment Administration, which had connections to the Department of Agriculture in Washington, D.C., knew about these things and his opinions were respected.

"Don't you think America's going to get into it sooner or later, though?" That was my brother Jim.

"I hope that never happens," Uncle Eph responded. "What happens over in Europe is not any affair of ours."

"Eph," Aunt Dorothy said, "it's Thanksgiving. Let's not talk about such grim things!"

We youngsters in the kitchen had lost interest by then. I was just in second grade and hadn't begun studying geography yet, so Europe was nothing more to me than a place on the map that hung in the classroom at school.

The meal ended and the men retired to the sitting room where they put up a card table and played euchre while the women cleaned up the dishes and put away and divvied up the leftovers to take home.

Now was the time for the real fun, when all of the grandchildren's names, written on slips of paper, were put into a bowl so we could draw them to see who would give to whom at Christmas.

Jim and the older cousins became restless, so they bundled up and took a walk around the farm; Eddie and I and our younger cousins took up residence under the dining room table to play, the only spot we could find where we wouldn't be underfoot and in anyone's way. The littlest ones began to get

Grandpa McCormick may have been the head of his household, but I believe Grandma was the true center of the family. Here she is with daughters and daughters-in-law (from left): Aunt Doris, Mother, Aunt Lucy, Grandma — in the center, of course! — Aunt Midah, Aunt Mildred, and Aunt Dorothy.

sleepy after awhile, and just as dusk was beginning to settle it was time to go. Hugs and kisses were exchanged along with "See you Christmas dinner" or "See you on Sunday" and we got into our cars and headed for home and the cow milking and livestock feeding that accompanied the end of every day on a farm.

"Emmy," Dad said as we pulled out of Grandpa's driveway, "I'm so full I don't think I'll ever be hungry again!" Mother just smiled. She knew better.

% % % % %

I woke up a little later than usual the next morning, even though Eddie and I had been tucked into our beds soon after the light supper of leftovers we'd had the evening before. Dad, Jim, and Don were already out at work around the farm; Mother moved around the kitchen getting her list ready for her weekly shopping trip into town on Saturday, and every now and then she sighed. Thanksgiving was just plain tiring, and the combination of the hunting and game-dressing the men did, the cooking and baking and cleaning up the women did, and the too-much play and too-much food (and in my case, too many Parker House rolls) the children indulged in, had everyone rubbing their eyes with fatigue.

% % % % %

Thanksgiving weekend marked the beginning of the Christmas baking season, and the next few weeks would be busy ones for Mother.

First on the list of baking projects was fruitcake. It was baked in the tube pan she used for angel-food cakes, which resulted in a lot of fruitcake to be enjoyed for quite a while.

And enjoy we did; unlike many fruitcakes that are so derided these days, Mother's were heavenly, dense confections loaded with nuts and jewel-like fruits. Once baked and cooled, the cake was then wrapped in cheesecloth that Mother moistened with a wee bit of brandy, the only alcoholic beverage that ever crossed the threshold of our home. The cake took at least three weeks to age properly, with occasional retouches of the brandy, thus the early start on it.

Nothing, but nothing, though, compared to coming home from school the day Mother had baked hermits and sniffing the aroma of our favorite Christmas cookie wafting through the house. These cookies weren't what you'd call particularly "Christmassy," as they had no festive decorations, but this was the only time of year Mother made them. The lingering spicy-citrusy scent was almost cruel, though, because by the time we got home the hermits were already packed up and hidden, with perhaps a half-dozen or so left on a plate for us kids to much on. Mice weren't a problem, but "pantry rats" were. Mother had learned years before that her oldest son was seriously addicted to hermits and that if they weren't tucked safely away there wouldn't be any left for holiday visitors.

Jim was not to be deterred, though, because in his opinion, the only thing better than Mother's hermits were Mother's hermits hunted, found, and snarfed on the sly. His instincts were unerring, and in the true tradition of younger siblings, as we got older we gleefully followed his lead and participated in the search and seizure mission.

Despite our persistence — and our success, for not a year went by that the stash wasn't found — we knew the value of conservation and were careful to not eat them all too quickly. Mother knew we would find them, regardless of her best efforts, but she also knew we knew that once they were gone, they were gone. Our mother was a creature of habit, and she made one and only one batch of hermits a year, and that never changed.

On the first Friday of December, three weeks after Thanksgiving, Aunt Edna, Mother's brother Ray's wife, came over. It was candy-making day, one of my favorites. Aunt Edna and Mother alternated kitchens from year to year, and this year was our turn. The two women always got an early start, right after morning chores and the children were off to school, but they were always still at it when I got home and I would get to "help," usually by "testing" a few pieces — for quality-control purposes, of course.

Each woman provided her own special ingredients, but the order of the day followed strict tradition. First, they made divinity, concocting the fluffy white mounds and topping them off with either a red or green maraschino cherry half. Next came pecan rolls. The mixture was carefully monitored and cooked to just the right consistency (candy thermometers were unheard of in our homes), cooled, then shaped into logs and rolled in chopped pecans.

Mother and Aunt Edna then turned their attention to another favorite, fondant drops dipped in bittersweet chocolate and crowned with an English walnut half. Last, but definitely not least, was the fudge. I practically drooled as I surveyed the large pans of candy, one chocolate, one vanilla, and one peanut butter. These were cut into one-inch squares and tucked into separate storage containers to keep the different flavors from intermingling. At the end of the day the fruits of their labors were divided between the two cooks so each would have a supply for her own household.

I loved watching my mother and aunt as they worked because I saw a side of them that was seldom revealed. The two were like girls, giggling and laughing while they stirred, tested, poured, molded, and decorated the delicacies. It was a happy beginning for the Christmas season, a time when guests dropped by frequently and Mother would proudly present them with one of her lovely plates full of goodies to nibble along with steaming cups of tea.

Saturday came and went, a standard chores-and-farm-work day for the men, chores and shopping in Vincennes for Mother and me. Sunday began as usual, with Dad and Mother up early for their morning chores, then all of us getting into the car and heading to church. Grandpa and Grandma were coming over for dinner afterward, and Mother tucked a roast and some potatoes into the oven before we left so the meal would be ready when we returned.

By the time dinner was over, though, all sense of normalcy was gone. The grown-ups huddled around the radio in our living room, quiet and pale. Instead of the usual Sunday-afternoon musical programs, newscasters talked with urgent voices about an attack on a place called Pearl Harbor by a country called Japan. This had no more meaning for me than did the dinner conversation on Thanksgiving about Europe, but I could tell by the faces of my parents, grandparents, and aunt and uncle that something very bad had happened, and Jim and Don also looked serious and concerned. Suddenly, the war that Uncle Eph had claimed just four weeks ago had nothing to do with our country had everything to do with our country. The mood in the house was so grim that it made even Eddie and me uneasy.

He and I were young children, though, and by the next day we had more important things to occupy our minds than a thing called war. Christmas was coming and we needed to focus on being as good as possible so Santa would be sure to visit us. We didn't make much in the way of wish lists, trusting Santa to bring us whatever we wanted.

Two more weeks went by, and on Saturday morning before Christmas Dad and Jim went out to a wooded area on our farm to select and cut the Christmas tree, with Don, Eddie, and me tagging along so we could offer our opinions on the best choice. Once the critical decision was made, the tree was cut and brought to the house, placed in the front room in its holder full of water, and Mother went to work on it, hanging the ornaments somewhat haphazardly, wherever she thought they might fit. Tinsel received equally little care, simply tossed randomly on the branches. Tree-decorating was never Mother's forte, but we thought it was magical and that's all that mattered.

On Christmas Eve Eddie climbed into bed with me. Being the only daughter, I had a bedroom to myself while my three brothers shared theirs, and because my room was right next to the front room — and the tree, Santa's destination — Eddie always begged me to let him sleep in my room on that night so he would be closer to the presents that would be there in the morning.

Our gifts were nothing spectacular by today's standards, but we didn't really expect all that much and were tickled with whatever we got. Our parents had always been frugal and practical and were not ones to shower their children with an overabundance of goodies. Jim and Don got things like new gloves and hats that would keep them warm as they worked outside during the winter, and new ties to wear to church on Sundays. Eddie got a toy truck to add to his collection of miniature farm equipment.

My favorite gifts that year were some beautiful outfits for the doll I had received the previous summer while I was recuperating from viral pneumonia. I'd had two other dolls, a rubber one I had carried around as a toddler until she wore out, and the other a baby doll with a stuffed cloth body, plaster hands and feet, and a plaster head with the hair painted on and eyes that opened and closed. She was the size of an actual newborn baby and often wore the booties and sleepers Eddie had outgrown early in his life. This new doll, though, was something else, a lovely eighteen-inch-tall creature with fully movable arms and legs and real blond hair fashioned in the pompadour style that was so popular in the early 1940s, covered with a tiny snood. I called her Betty because one of

My best girlfriend and cousin, Alice Ann (right) and me. I'm holding my beloved Betty and hoping I'll find some new frocks for her from Mrs. Claus under the Christmas tree.

my aunts had commented that she looked like Betty Grable, the movie star. The only clothing my Betty had worn for the past several months was the lacy bridal attire she came with, so I was thrilled when I unwrapped the gorgeous new frocks that Mrs. Claus (AKA Aunt Edna) had made for her.

※ ※ ※ ※ ※

My parents did their best to make that holiday season a happy one, but despite their efforts, tension hung over the house like a fog. We may have been somewhat insulated from the rest of the world in our little corner of southern Indiana, but this war that our country had been pulled into earlier in the month was going to drastically alter our lives.

Shortly after the attack on Pearl Harbor, my dad took a new job as national chief of the Corn and Soybean Division of the Commodity Credit Corporation in Washington, D.C. He moved to the nation's capital to take up that position right after New Year's Day. The problem was, we all would be staying behind. The farm was precious to our family, but now all farms were valuable national assets during this time of war, and Mother had to stay to run ours.

Because Dad had worked away from home pretty much since I was born, we had been used to seeing him only on weekends. Now we wouldn't see him even that often, and we were to find out that aside from trips back for holidays and other special occasions, Dad would be for the most part an absentee figure for the next four years. My childhood memory doesn't recall too much about his departure on the Baltimore & Ohio (B&O) train that winter, but I do remember my mother crying. Eddie and I had never seen her do that and we were upset too.

Over the next four years the world changed and so did I. In that time I went from being just a "little kid" to the threshold of adolescence and young womanhood. It was hard without my dad around, but although he was absent in body, he was never far away in spirit. He wrote faithfully to Mother and just as faithfully to me, and his words provided the guidance I needed in those formative years.

I grew, I matured, and I learned. And like my country during that tumultuous era, I became stronger and more independent than I could ever have imagined.

Who cares about getting cold when you have a horse-drawn sled to take you through the snow? With older brother Don at the reins, little brother Eddie and I are ready for a ride!

CHAPTER 10

The Fabric of Life

*T*he fibers that comprise the fabric of our lives are all too often heartbreakingly fragile. I learned that the hard way when my dear mother began to slip away into the unbearable haze of dementia that was the onset of Alzheimer's disease.

Our father had not long before succumbed to Parkinson's disease, he unwillingly leaving the care of his beloved bride to his four offspring, my brothers and me. Mercifully for Mother, we doubted that she was aware of his passing, for in the last years of Dad's illness she had drifted further and irretrievably away from us.

As the four of us contemplated the future of our widowed and increasingly mentally incompetent mother we decided the best immediate course was to keep her in the house she had called "home" for more than fifty years. We arranged for her care and she remained there until the last six months of her life.

It was at that point that I, the only daughter, became the de facto keeper of most of the items accumulated in our parents' life together. My brothers didn't know what to do with those things, so it was up to me to sift through their belongings.

I left Mother's personal possessions for last. I methodically emptied her chest of drawers and dresser, arranging the items in neat stacks on the bed. Here an embroidered handkerchief with her initials; there a nightgown, never worn, saved for "special" — I made a mental note to take that to her at the nursing home the next day so she could wear it and look pretty.

As I pulled the last garments from the bottom drawer of the chest, a glimpse of bright color nestled within the folds of some tissue paper caught my eye. Unwrapping it, I found a small, toddler-sized dress that Mother had lovingly tucked away. I held it up and marveled over it: the tiny lacy collar, the fine, even stitches, the delicate tucking, the warm blush of the peach-colored fabric. Into my mind flashed a photograph I had seen recently, as my brothers and I had gone through the family albums, of me in this same little garment.

My goodness, I thought, *what possessed her to keep this?* Mother had stitched so many frocks for me, the only girl in a brood of four. What special memory, which singular occasion caused her to treasure this particular one? I couldn't ask her and would never know for sure, but I as I sat there with the little dress in my lap, sniffing the faint lavender of the sachet that had been tucked in with it, I let my imagination wander. Perhaps it was simply the specialness of a warm day in spring that lingered in Mother's memory, one of those wispy moments in time when she did something simply because she wanted to.

I closed my eyes and dreamed, and in my dream I put myself in Mother's shoes, the ones she wore when this wonderful heirloom came to be.

※ ※ ※ ※ ※

"Looks likes it's going to be a nice day," Clarence said as he rolled out of bed shortly after sunrise. "Mm-hmm," Emma murmured as she snuggled into the covers for a few minutes longer, knowing that her husband liked to do some morning chores — milking and feeding livestock — before eating breakfast. Besides, she had already been up a couple of times during the night with little Eddie. At four months of age he was a sweetheart of a baby, but needed to be nursed every three to four hours, an exhausting schedule for his mother whose days as a farm wife left little time for napping. This was Saturday, though, and the schedule was different from the rest of the week.

As Emma lay in bed, listening to the birds singing outside and Clarence softly whistling as he dressed, she considered how nice it was when the weekends rolled around. Clarence worked away from their farm home during the week, and from the time his car turned out of their driveway on Monday morning until he returned on Friday evenings in time for supper, she had her hands full with their older children: twelve-year-old Jimmie, seven-year-old Donnie, and little Lorene, still a baby herself at twenty-two months. Clarence's return and the change in routine were a welcome break from Emma's weekday life of getting the older boys off to school and tending to the household responsibilities single-handed.

This Saturday, however, was particularly special and she smiled to herself as she thought of the shopping trip in town in the afternoon. She would be accompanied only by the baby, as the older boys would be helping their dad with farm work and their neighbor's daughter, Dorothy Jane, was coming to tend to Lorene. Dorothy Jane helped around the house during the week, so Emma knew she could count on her to clean up the noontime dinner dishes and have supper started by the time she returned.

"Maybe I'll even have her bake the Sunday cake, too," Emma mused as she sat on the side of the bed and stretched. That would be one less thing to get done before she drove the family car the seven miles into town. Thank goodness she no longer had to travel by horse and buggy as she had when she was growing up. The travel time would have been prohibitive for just a two- or three-hour shopping trip.

While she dressed and fixed her hair, Emma's mind raced as she ticked off chores to be done while she was gone and made a mental list of her shopping needs. So much of their food was homegrown that for the most part all she had to purchase at the grocery store were staples like flour, sugar, and salt. A few additions always found their way onto the list, of course, depending on what she planned to bake the next week. Did she have enough raisins and brown sugar for her fantastic cookies? What about baking powder or soda? Better check on spices, too. Clarence needed the family's only car to get to his job in the city, so it wouldn't do to forget something necessary because it would have to wait until the next weekly trip to town, a good reason to make a complete list.

But it wasn't groceries that lit up her mood that Saturday morning in May 1936. No, there wasn't anything very exciting about buying food supplies. The treat for her that day was knowing that she was going to Gimbel Bond's department store. Emma was talented and creative, with a flair for the piano and organ. But when she wasn't making music, she loved few things more than sewing and hand-work — crocheting, tatting, and embroidery — especially now that she had an adorable little blue-eyed, blond-haired daughter who gave her the perfect excuse for indulging her passion for needle-and-thread projects.

For weeks now Emma had been musing over a special dress to make for Lorene, maybe something summery since the weather would soon be warming up. She wasn't sure what color she wanted, or how she wanted the dress to look in the end; she would know the right thing when she saw it. *Better get fabric for a little petticoat, too.* This would be a Sunday dress, Emma decided. Sunday go-to-church dresses were fancier and a lot more fun to make than everyday dresses.

Emma's practical angel tapped on her shoulder, though, and she figured while she was at the store she could see what she could find for a couple of aprons. Nice big aprons saved wear and tear on everyday house dresses, and washing and ironing those was a lot easier than doing so with a whole dress. Laundry was hard enough work as it was in those days before automatic washing machines, even with Dorothy Jane helping out, what with loads of baby diapers along with what the other children wore, plus the crisply starched shirts Clarence wore to work. Yes, a couple of new aprons would do well indeed.

Checking on Eddie, Emma was gratified to see that he was still sound asleep. That gave her a few minutes to go over how much money she had to spend in town. The country was in the early stages of recovering from the Great Depression and money was scarce everywhere, which was why Clarence had taken the job away from the farm. Emma had a thriving chicken-and-egg business, though, and the income she made from selling the eggs her chickens laid provided for her indulgence in pretties for herself and her little daughter.

Emma's German background made her frugal by nature. "Wouldn't it be better to tuck this money away, just in case?" she had asked Clarence once. "Absolutely not," he had replied, giving her a kiss. "You work hard for that money, and I want you to feel you can spend it as you see fit. Besides, you know I want my 'girls' to look like princesses when we go out!" He was always proud of his lovely blue-eyed bride's appearance when they went to Sunday school and church at Trinity Methodist, and took great pleasure in showing off his little daughter decked out in frills and bows.

Besides, Emma's sewing projects provided welcome respite from her daily chores. How relaxing it was to be able to sew three or four afternoons a week after the dinner dishes were done and before it was time to do end-of-day chores and start supper, and so gratifying to see the finished product: a new shirt for one of the boys — they outgrew them so fast! — a new apron that, despite its serviceability, still brightened up a day in the kitchen; or a lovely new dress for herself or Lorene.

As she bustled around that Saturday morning, time flew. With Dorothy Jane's help, the noon meal of fried pork chops, mashed potatoes and gravy, home-canned green beans, and cold home-canned tomatoes (Clarence's favorite) was prepared and served right on time. Some pie was leftover from yesterday's baking so she hadn't needed to take the time to bake that, not that it took her very long to whip up a pie; she had made so many she could almost put them together in her sleep.

Emma tucked Eddie securely into the front passenger seat of the car, then got in and turned the key in the ignition. It always seemed strange, even after all these years, to drive into town by herself. August Bobe, her father, had always kept a loving but close eye on his daughters after the death of his wife when the children were quite young, and to venture far from home unescorted was unthinkable when she was growing up. Clarence, however, encouraged her to be self-sufficient and independent, in large part because he wasn't around during the week to take care of things. Emma sighed; she would have preferred to not have to be so independent. She wasn't totally without support and resources, as her sisters and brothers all lived within a few miles; but she would have rather had her husband at home more.

She put the car into gear and was halfway down the driveway when Donnie ran up to the car. "Mother," he panted, "don't forget to buy raisins! You promised you'd make cookies this week." She smiled and reached through the window to smooth his tousled red-blond hair. "I won't forget the raisins," she said. "But you be sure to mind your father and help out, or there won't be any cookies for a month."

She smiled to herself as she continued down toward the road. Her boys were good boys; no need to worry about their doing what was needed. Young Jim had shouldered so much responsibility since Clarence had taken the town job. It seemed they had to grow up so fast, she thought with some regret; she herself had had to grow up fast after the loss of her mother when she was a little girl.

In town, Emma sped through her necessary errands and headed to Gimbel Bond's yard goods section where she took her time examining the rainbow of fabrics on the shelves. A crisp light-green and yellow plaid for one apron and a colorful pink calico for another were already cut and folded in her stack, along with bright rickrack for trimming the edges. Now she cast a critical eye over a bolt of light blue gauze, then a sunshine yellow swiss. Both fabrics were lovely, but neither was quite what she had in her mind for Lorene's special dress. Eddie began to fuss, even though Emma had stopped in the ladies' lounge to nurse him just a short while before, and she shifted him from arm to arm in an attempt to keep him happy for just a bit longer. He wasn't having any of it, though, and she began to think she would have to abandon the search for the perfect fabric until another day. She set Eddie on the counter, taking care that he couldn't roll or squirm off, and fished in her purse for her wallet. That was when she spotted a sliver of peachy-pink, a roll of cotton voile almost hidden at the bottom of a stack of bolts on the counter waiting to be put away.

"That one," she said, pointing to it. "May I see it?" The clerk obliged and pulled it out for her examination. It was perfect. Emma could picture the little garment in her mind's eye, a simple flared line of a dress with short, puffed sleeves and delicate lacy trim on the round collar. Lorene would look like an angel in it! The clerk measured out the required yardage and the peach voile was added to the bundle of apron fabric. Brown paper and string were tied around the parcel and away Emma went, and just in time because Eddie was letting her know in no uncertain terms by then that he was through with shopping for the day.

Back in the car, once she had Eddie quieted and asleep on the car seat beside her, Emma drove toward home, humming her favorite hymns all the way. She could hardly wait to show the fabric to Dorothy Jane, who took equal pride in dolling up "their" little girl. The young woman always had good ideas about Lorene's dresses and sometimes helped with the sewing. She was barely eighteen but farm girls learned to sew at an early age. That skill was as important as being able to cook and bake because good, serviceable ready-to-wear dresses were hard to find — much less afford — in the small farming community.

Emma turned off the gravel country road that ran in front of her house and checked her wristwatch. She had made good time, and she breathed a sigh of relief that she would have a little while to rest before the evening activities began.

Saturday night was bath night. Clarence hauled the big metal tub into the kitchen while Emma heated water on the cook stove. Jimmie and Donnie always fussed over who got to get in the water first, but with their parents' intervention the dispute was settled and the baths were taken. Emma noticed the boys' hair was getting a little long around their ears and necks, so she sat them down for a trim, another Saturday ritual that took place about once a month. Clarence didn't need her services there as he got his hair cut at the barber shop in town during the work week.

When the boys were finished and sent off to get ready for bed, Clarence emptied the tub and Emma refilled it with fresh water. She got Lorene cleaned up and settled into her nightie. Then it was her own turn, and she bathed and washed her hair so she would look nice for Sunday socializing and church. Emma's hair was a lovely honey-blonde color, and she wore it neck length, which showed off its natural wave. As she sang little Lorene to sleep, Emma wound a lock of the child's hair around her finger and smiled. Her daughter seemed to have inherited her wave. Emma was happy about that; it didn't matter that the older boys had their father's stick-straight hair because they didn't care how it looked anyway. As for baby Eddie, it was too soon to tell.

As the scrubbed and shampooed family settled into their beds that night, they didn't have any difficulty falling asleep.

A day of fresh air and physical labor, followed by a soothing bath, were potent sleeping aides.

Sunday dawned warmer than usual for May. A few clouds lurked on the western horizon and it felt like rain was in the air, and Emma and Clarence hoped for a good, soaking shower. The newly planted fields of corn, wheat, and soybeans would benefit, as would the vegetable and flower gardens.

Sunday may have been designated a day of rest by the Bible, but on the farm there was no such thing as a day of total rest. Chickens, cows, and hogs didn't take days off — ever — and Emma and Clarence saw to their usual morning chores. By nine A.M. the little ones were dressed in their Sunday clothes and Jimmie and Donnie were inspected for combed hair, clean nails, and spotless clothes. With an admonition to them to *stay* clean, Emma and Clarence got into their church clothing. Giving herself a quick glance in the mirror of her dresser, Emma donned her hat and stuck a hatpin through it to keep it in place, and away they went.

It was past noon by the time their family car turned into the driveway at home and everyone was hungry. Dinner had been put into the oven before they left, so it was more or less done and ready to set out on the table. Clarence's parents were there, as well as the pastor and his wife. While the men discussed crops and the news and the women chatted about their gardens, Emma quickly laid out the meal. Everyone took their seats and Clarence invited the pastor to offer the blessing. The food was passed and Emma happily accepted compliments on how tasty everything was. The children ate quietly with no complaints about anything. The rule was that you were required to eat all of whatever you put it on your plate. Neither waste nor piggishness was tolerated and children learned to be judicious about their food selections.

Clean plates were the standard (and made the cleanup easier after the meal).

By two o'clock the guests had departed and it was naptime for Emma and the little ones. Clarence dozed in his big, comfortable living-room chair, the half-read Sunday paper in his lap. The older boys amused themselves outside, where they tossed a baseball back and forth.

The less-busy time Sundays offered enabled the family to recharge and enjoy quiet time together, a time they treasured. Outside distractions were few. There was no point in slipping into town for anything because, except for the movie theater that didn't open until evening, all the stores and businesses were closed, and the only time they "ate out" was when they had dinner at a relative's home.

※ ※ ※ ※ ※

Two weeks passed and Lorene's dress was finished. It fit perfectly and looked adorable on her. The average farmer in those days valued strong sons — the more the better — when the work was so labor-intensive, and Clarence McCormick was no exception. Nevertheless, the word "average" did not apply to him, and he puffed with pride any time he had a chance to show off his adored daughter.

"Dance for Dad," he said as Lorene paraded in her beautiful new frock. "Let me see you twirl." Lorene was more than willing to oblige such an appreciative audience and spun until she dropped into a dizzy pile on the floor, giggling. She wasn't two years old yet, but she was smart enough to know she had her adored Daddy twisted tightly around her little finger, right where she wanted him.

"Clarence, you'll spoil her," Emma scolded gently.

"Oh, Emmy, you can't spoil a baby," he said, bussing her cheek and ignoring the mutterings of "Princess" that came from Jim and Donnie as they passed by on their way to the kitchen. "Besides," Clarence added, "I only get to see her on weekends."

Emma was all too painfully aware of that and turned to go into the kitchen so he wouldn't see the hurt in her eyes. She knew Clarence treasured his family; but he also was an ambitious man who loved his work and who wanted to see how far he could go. She was proud of him and supported him, but even though the management of the farm went smoothly with the help of hired hands and she had no problems running it, it was not what she had bargained for when she got married. She wanted her husband home with her, and often her disappointment was hard to conceal.

※ ※ ※ ※ ※

Over the years Emma made countless items of clothing for her children, an almost endless task as they grew older and taller. At least the boys could wear hand-me-downs, but Lorene seemed to need a whole new wardrobe every six months, even when the clothes were made with plenty of "grow room." Just when Emma thought she had everything covered — literally — Lorene's knees would be popping out under the hems of her dresses, and the waistlines had moved uncomfortably close to her armpits. Emma never minded, though, because the time she spent with colorful fabrics and trims and tucks and laces and ruffles was more like play than work to her.

Emma crafted many special garments for her little girl. She had a canny eye for style and color and each of her daughter's dresses was unusual and attention-getting. Who

111

but Emma McCormick would have dared consider putting a russet-brown fabric on a young child? She remembered making that dress with its white Peter Pan collar.

"Stop fidgeting, Strutsie," Emma said to the squirmy six-year-old during one of the fittings. "I'll stick a pin in you."

"I can't, Mother! You're already sticking me!" Lorene answered. She loved her pretty clothes, but right then she wanted to be outside playing with Eddie.

The dress was finished and despite the dark "grown-up" hue, it was perfect on the rosy-cheeked, fair-complexioned girl — just as her mother knew it would be. It was quickly outgrown though, and Emma moved on to create other works of art for her daughter, like the one made of medium-blue linen-like fabric with a hand-embroidered bodice trim for eight-year-old Lorene. The headaches and eyestrain from hours spent on the embroidery were well worth it when she saw the end result, complete with the crowning touch of a matching hair bow for Lorene's blonde locks.

Emma's skill in the art of sewing was never more apparent than in the winter of 1944 when ten-year-old Lorene wore a masterpiece of ruby-red velveteen for her solo of "Away in a Manger" in the Christmas program at church. The dress was stunning in its simplicity of a simple round neckline and gently gathered skirt, and Lorene proudly wore it for the family photo taken that year.

※ ※ ※ ※ ※

During Emma's girlhood, daughters accepted their parents' dictums unquestionably. Times had changed, though, and as Lorene grew up she developed a mind of her own, one that constantly questioned. She wasn't rebellious by nature, but she did begin to succumb to some peer pressure at school, where a few of the girls *bought* their dresses ready to wear from the store, and she became less enthusiastic about wearing the homemade ones her mother so painstakingly stitched. As mothers and daughters will, they butted heads on more than one occasion on this topic. Emma was forced to acknowledge the girl's advance toward young womanhood and independence. She was, after all, the product of two very

Peach-colored voile, lace, and ribbons, stitched together with yards and yards of love.

strong-minded parents and that independence was hard-wired into her makeup.

Things came to a head when Lorene, facing her eighth-grade graduation, insisted she wanted a store-bought dress. Nothing was wrong with what Mother made, but she would have to wait as long as *two weeks* until it was ready to wear. Emma's sense of frugality and what constituted true quality finally was overruled by her daughter's pleadings. Thus, one fine Saturday morning in late March, mother and daughter went to town to look for the much-longed-for dress. *Goodness,* Emma sniffed to herself, *these seams will fall apart at the first sneeze!* Lorene, on the other hand, was dazzled by the selection of garments she could wear *now,* and before long fell in love with a cotton dress with tiny red checks and a pretty bodice. It was unlike anything she had ever owned, and even if the quality wasn't as good (she knew what her mother was thinking!) just having it made Lorene feel very grown-up.

※ ※ ※ ※ ※

By the time Lorene reached her teens, she had begun to sew, too, in great part because of her home economics classes in school and her participation in 4-H. (In rural communities in those days, 4-H was not an option; you just did it.) Lorene's earliest 4-H projects were the most basic: hand- and machine-hemmed linen tea towels the first year; an apron the second year. The girl could barely suppress her yawns; tea towels and aprons — where in the world was the fun in that! Nevertheless, she learned the basics of sewing and began to understand her mother's scorn for ready-to-wear. By the time the third year in 4-H came around, and when Lorene made her first dress, she was hooked and there was no turning back. Her mother

Mother was incredibly talented with a needle and thread and created many imaginative outfits for me, such as the little coat and cap ensemble I'm wearing here.

gave opinions on fabric selections, but those were out-the-window in favor of the Lorene's own choices.

The sewing bug had bitten her hard, and for the next forty years, if for no other reason than the joy of creating something of quality no one else had, she constructed her own clothing, even making her own elaborate gown for her wedding at age twenty-one.

※ ※ ※ ※ ※

Oh, dear, how long have I been sitting here? I wondered. It wasn't dark, but the sun had sunk lower in the sky, and there I sat on the edge of my mother's bed, the little peach-colored dress still in my lap.

Little Eddie — no longer little by now, of course — was the last child my parents had. All four of us had grown up, gone to college, married, and had families of our own. Our father's ambitions had taken him as far as the White House, where he had been Undersecretary of Agriculture for President Truman.

Meantime, my mother, for the most part, had stayed back home on the farm where she raised her children and tended her flower and vegetable gardens, taking pleasure in watching young things grow and bloom. And although she and I had our differences — perhaps because in some ways we were so much alike? — she continued to conceive and craft so many lovely items for me.

In time, however, the tables turned. Failing eyesight made threading needles difficult for her, and the small stitches were harder to pick apart when a seam was a bit crooked. I had inherited her passion for sewing, and ultimately my skills began to surpass those of the master — my mother. I began sewing for her.

Now it was I who said, "Don't fidget or I'll stick you."
And she would just smile, as if recalling a day of russet-toned
fabric on a six-year-old.

It was bittersweet, this passing of a torch. Yet it was
thrilling for me, and for her also, I believe, to realize the gift
we had brought to each other. My mother's love was woven
and stitched into each dress she made for me. My love for her
was evident and emblazoned in every stitch I sewed for her.

And I realized that such is the fabric of life: giving,
taking, and sharing.

Recipes

RECIPES

BAKING POWDER BISCUITS

My mother could have saved herself some biscuit-making grief if only she'd had this recipe or the one following.

> 2 cups sifted flour
> 4 teaspoons baking powder
> ½ teaspoon salt
> 4–6 tablespoons fat (cold)
> ⅔ – ¾ cup milk

Sift together flour, baking powder, and salt. Combine these dry ingredients and the fat by rubbing them between the fingers and thumb. To do this, pick up a portion of fat and flour, drop back in the bowl, and so on. (A pastry blender could be used for this process.) Continue until the mixture is fairly smooth and has the general appearance of coarse meal.

Add milk and stir for about 20 seconds. Turn dough onto a lightly floured board and knead for about 20 strokes. If the dough begins to stick, sprinkle a little more flour on the board.

Shape dough into a ball and pat or roll into about a ¾-inch thickness. Cut with a floured biscuit cutter and place on greased or ungreased baking sheet. The biscuits will have a more uniform shape if lifted from board to pan by a spatula or knife. Bake at 425 degrees for about 12–15 minutes, or until golden brown. (Note: The pan of biscuits may be refrigerated as long as 3 hours before baking.)

Mother always enjoyed a bite of something sweet after a family dinner.

MILE-HIGH BISCUITS

3 cups sifted flour

2 tablespoons sugar

4½ teaspoons baking powder

¾ teaspoon cream of tartar

¾ teaspoon salt

¾ cup shortening

1 egg, beaten

1 cup milk

Sift together flour, sugar, baking powder, cream of tartar, and salt into a bowl. Cut in shortening with a pastry blender or two knives until mixture resembles coarse meal. Combine egg and milk and add to flour mixture all at once, stirring with a fork just enough to make a soft dough that sticks together.

Turn onto a lightly floured surface and knead lightly 15 times, then roll to 1-inch thickness. Cut with floured 2-inch cutter and place about 1 inch apart on an ungreased baking sheet.

Bake in 425 degree oven 12–15 minutes or until golden brown; serve immediately. Makes 16 biscuits.

PLAIN LOAF CAKE

*My early 4-H baking projects were simple cakes. The recipes
may be simple but the end results are hard to beat.*

2 cups sifted flour

2 teaspoons baking powder

¼ teaspoon salt

½ cup butter, room temperature

1 cup sugar

1 teaspoon vanilla

2 eggs, separated

⅔ cup milk

Grease and flour an 8-by-4-inch loaf pan or an 8-inch cake
pan. Preheat oven to 350 degrees.

Sift flour, baking powder, and salt together in a bowl; set
aside. Cream butter until smooth, then gradually add sugar
and continue creaming until mixture is fluffy. Lightly beat
egg yolks and add to the butter mixture. Add vanilla. In a
separate bowl, beat egg whites until stiff but not dry.

Alternately add flour mixture and milk alternately to the
butter mixture. Beat until well combined, about 1 minute.
Gently fold in the beaten egg whites.

Pour batter into prepared pan and bake 45 minutes (30
minutes for a cake pan) or until done. Turn cake out of pan
and allow to cool on a rack.

PLAIN BUTTER CAKE

½ cup butter

1½ cups sugar

1 teaspoon vanilla

2 eggs, lightly beaten

1 cup milk

2⅞ cups sifted flour

2⅔ teaspoons baking powder

1 teaspoon salt

Grease and flour an 8-by-4-inch loaf pan or an 8-inch cake pan. Preheat oven to 350 degrees.

Cream butter and half the sugar; add vanilla. Sift together the flour, baking powder and salt. Add the flour and milk alternately to the butter mixture and mix thoroughly. Combine eggs and the remaining sugar and beat on medium speed for about 5 minutes; add to the batter.

Pour batter into the prepared pan and bake 45 minutes if in a loaf pan, 30 minutes if in a cake pan, or until done.

LADY BALTIMORE CAKE

*Aunt Helen had a special way of making her famous
Lady Baltimore Cake and a streamlined way of
writing out her recipe.*

Beat 6 egg whites and ¼ teaspoon cream of tartar until stiff.

Sift together 3 times 2 ½ cups cake flour, ¼ teaspoon salt, and
3 teaspoons baking powder.

Roll in flour ½ cup chopped nuts and 18 maraschino cherries,
drained and chopped fine.

Cream ½ cup butter and 1 ½ cups sugar. Add to this ¼ cup
cherry juice, ½ cup milk, and 1 teaspoon vanilla.

Combine all ingredients, folding egg whites in last. Pour
batter into a greased and floured 9-by-13-inch pan and bake
at 350 degrees until cake tests done.

Remove from pan and let cool, then frost with Seven-Minute
Frosting (recipe follows).

SEVEN-MINUTE FROSTING

⅞ cup sugar

3 tablespoons cold water

1 egg white (unbeaten)

¼ teaspoon salt

¼ teaspoon baking powder

½ teaspoon vanilla

Bring water in the bottom of a double boiler to a rolling simmer. Combine all ingredients except vanilla in the top part of the double boiler; beat with a rotary beater. Cook seven minutes over the simmering water, beating constantly. Remove the top of the boiler from the heat and add the vanilla. Continue beating until the mixture is thick enough to spread. The frosting should not be hot when it is put on the cake.

If the mixture shows signs of hardening in the pan before it can be spread on the cake, beat in a few drops of hot water or lemon juice.

If the mixture refuses to thicken enough to spread after long beating, place back over hot water over a low flame and beat with a wire whisk until there is a slight scraping sound at the edges of the pan, which indicates that sugar crystals are forming. Remove from the hot water and beat again until thick enough to spread.

APPLESAUCE CAKE

⅔ cup butter

1 cup sugar

2 eggs, well beaten

1 cup applesauce, unsweetened

½ cup raisins

2 cups sifted flour

1 teaspoon baking soda

½ teaspoon nutmeg

1 teaspoon cinnamon

¼ teaspoon ground cloves

Grease and flour an 8-inch cake pan. Preheat oven to 350 degrees.

Cream butter and sugar until fluffy. Add eggs, then applesauce, and mix thoroughly. Sift together the dry ingredients and add to the applesauce mixture. Fold in the raisins.

Pour batter into prepared pan and bake 30–40 minutes, or until cake tests done.

ANGEL FOOD CAKE

This was Mother's "signature" cake that she made for our birthdays, and only long after I became an adult did I discover her recipe had come from the Swan's Down Cake Flour box. Doesn't matter — Mother's secret is safe with me!

1¼	cups sifted cake flour
½	cup sugar
1½	cups (about 12) egg whites (at room temperature)
1¼	teaspoons cream of tartar
¼	teaspoon salt
1	teaspoon vanilla
¼	teaspoon almond extract
1⅓	cups sugar

Sift cake flour and ½ cup sugar together 4 times.

Combine egg whites, cream of tartar, salt, and flavorings in a large bowl and mix at high speed with an electric mixer or rotary beater until soft peaks form. Add the rest of the sugar in 4 additions, beating until blended after each addition.

Sift in flour mixture in 4 additions, folding in with a large spoon, turning bowl often.

Pour into ungreased 10-inch tube pan. Bake at 375 degrees 35–40 minutes. Cool cake in pan upside-down on cake rack, then remove from pan.

AUNT MARY'S DEVILS FOOD CAKE

This "recipt" (the old-fashioned term for "recipe") for Devil's Food Cake came from my great-aunt Mary, according to the scrap of paper that it's written on. Many times the recipes had no mixing or baking instructions. I guess the cooks thought that everyone knew how to finish them!

Beat 2 cups sugar and ½ cup softened butter. Add 3 egg yolks, one at a time, and beat again after each yolk addition. Then add 5 tablespoons cocoa dissolved in ½ cup hot coffee. Blend in 2 cups flour (or a little more) and 1 teaspoon soda dissolved in ½ cup sour milk. Fold in beaten egg whites. Pour into two greased and floured 9-inch cake pans or one 9-by-13-inch pan. Bake in 350 degrees preheated oven for 25 minutes or until cakes spring back when touched in the middle. Cool for 10 minutes then remove rounds from pans and cool on racks or leave the cake in the rectangular pan and cool on a wire rack. Frost with favorite frosting.

YELLOW ANGEL FOOD CAKE

Just about everyone knows that Angel Food Cake is probably the original "fat-free" dessert partly because it doesn't use the yolks of the eggs. So YELLOW Angel Food Cake? How can that be? (Hint: Use the yolks that weren't incorporated in the regular Angel Food Cake recipe!)

    ¼   teaspoon salt
    ¾   cup warm (tepid) water
    12 egg yolks
    1¼ cups sugar, sifted twice
    2   cups cake flour
        (sifted twice before measuring)
    ½   teaspoon vanilla
    ½   teaspoon lemon extract
    2   teaspoons baking powder

Grease and flour a 10-inch tube pan. Preheat oven to 350 degrees.

Add salt and warm water to egg yolks, beat until stiff enough to stand. Whip in sugar.

Fold flour in gradually (this is important); add flavorings, then baking powder. Pour batter into prepared pan and bake 50 minutes, or until done.

SPONGE CAKE

This was Mother's stand-by for strawberry shortcake.
No biscuits for her!

> 4 eggs, separated
> 1 cup sugar
> ¼ cup water or pineapple juice
> 1 cup flour
> 1 slightly heaping teaspoon baking powder

Grease and flour a 9-by-13-inch pan. Heat oven to 400 degrees.

Beat egg whites until stiff but not dry; set aside. Beat yolks, add sugar. Alternately add liquid and dry ingredients. Fold in egg whites.

Pour batter into pan and bake about 15 minutes, or until cake springs back when lightly touched.

LAZY DAISY OATMEAL CAKE

Surely an oatmeal cake could be
considered health food, right?

FOR THE CAKE:

1¼ cups boiling water

1 cup oats
(quick or old fashioned)

½ cup butter, softened

1 cup granulated sugar

⅓ cup chopped nuts

1 cup firmly packed
brown sugar

1 teaspoon vanilla

2 eggs

1½ cups sifted all-purpose flour

1 teaspoon soda

½ teaspoon salt

¾ teaspoon cinnamon

¼ teaspoon nutmeg

FOR THE FROSTING:

¼ cup butter, melted

½ cup firmly packed
brown sugar

3 tablespoons
half and half

¾ cup shredded coconut

For cake, pour boiling water over oats; cover and let stand 20 minutes. Beat butter until creamy; gradually add sugars and beat until fluffy. Blend in vanilla and eggs. Add oats mixture, mix well. Sift together flour, soda, salt, cinnamon, and nutmeg. Add to creamed mixture and mix well. Pour batter into greased and floured 9-inch square pan and bake at 350 degrees 35–40 minutes. Do not remove cake from pan.

For frosting, combine all ingredients. Spread evenly over cake. Broil until frosting becomes bubbly. Cake may be served warm or cold.

CHOCOLATE COOKIE CAKE

Just the name alone is enough to give me a sugar rush!

Sift together 1 cup flour, 1 cup sugar and ½ teaspoon salt. Bring just to a boil 1 stick butter or margarine, ½ cup water and 2 tablespoons cocoa; pour over flour mixture and combine. Add ¼ cup buttermilk, ½ teaspoon soda, ½ teaspoon vanilla, and 1 egg, beaten. Mix well and pour into greased jelly-roll pan. Bake at 375 degrees for 30 minutes.

While cake is baking, bring just to a boil ½ stick butter or margarine, 2 tablespoons cocoa and 3 tablespoons milk. Add ½ pound powdered sugar, ½ teaspoon vanilla and ½ cup chopped nuts. Beat mixture until smooth and pour over cake while hot.

Cut cake into 3-inch squares. Top with whipped cream, if desired.

FAMILY PIE

One hand full of forgiveness,

One heaping cupful of love,

A full pound of unselfishness,

Mixed together smoothly with complete faith in God.

Add 2 tablespoons of wisdom, one teaspoonful
of good nature for flavor, then sprinkle
generously with thoughtfulness!

This makes a wonderful family pie.

— author unknown

MOTHER'S APPLE PIE

The women in my family were the ultimate pie bakers,
and Mother was no exception.

FOR EMMA'S PERFECT PIE CRUST:

  4 cups unsifted all-purpose flour
      (lightly spooned into the cup)

  1 tablespoon sugar

  2 teaspoons salt

  1¾ cups vegetable shortening (not refrigerated;
      do not substitute lard, oil, or butter)

  ½ cup water

  1 tablespoon white or cider vinegar

  1 large egg

Combine first 3 ingredients in a bowl and mix well with fork until mixture is crumbly. An a small bowl beat together water, vinegar, and egg. Add to flour mixture and stir with fork just until moistened. Divide dough into 5 portions and shape each into a flat, round disk ready for rolling. Wrap each disk in waxed paper or plastic wrap and chill at least 30 minutes. (Each disk makes one large crust.) These may be refrigerated up to one week or frozen.

For Filling:

> 6 cups thinly sliced peeled apples
>
> 1 cup sugar
>
> 1 tablespoon cornstarch
>
> ½ teaspoon ground cinnamon
>
> ½ teaspoon ground nutmeg

Using enough pastry for a double-crust pie (2 disks as above) roll out one on a lightly floured surface and fit gently into a 9-inch pie plate. Combine apples, sugar, cornstarch, cinnamon, and nutmeg arrange mixture in the pastry-lined plate with apple mixture mounded somewhat in the center.

Roll out remaining pastry and cut into ½-inch strips. Interlace strips in crisscross fashion over filling to make a lattice top. Trip strips even with pie edge. Turn bottom crust up over ends of strips and press firmly to seal edge. Flute edge.

Bake at 400 degrees for 45 minutes or until apples are tender. Makes 6–8 servings.

MOTHER'S "LATER" APPLE PIE

A clever baker, my mother developed this superb recipe in her later years, one that's easy to make because it has no top crust and is more like a classic French tart.

Pastry for 8- or 9-inch pie

4 or 5 tart apples, peeled and chopped

½ cup sugar

1 teaspoon cinnamon

2 tablespoons flour

1–2 tablespoons butter

Arrange apples in pastry-lined pie plate. Combine sugar, cinnamon, and flour and spread over apples. Dot with butter. Bake at 375 degrees for 20 minutes or until apples are tender.

LEMON MERINGUE PIE

*This was from my aunt Midah (Dad's sister). I'm lucky
to have a book of her recipes, copied from pages
written in her own hand.*

- ¾ cup sugar
- 2 tablespoons cornstarch
-    Speck of salt
- 1 cup boiling water
- 4 tablespoons bottled lemon juice
     (or juice of 1 large lemon)
- 1 tablespoon butter
- 3 eggs, separated

Combine sugar, cornstarch, and salt in the top of a double boiler and mix well. Slowly add the boiling water and cook mixture over simmering water, stirring constantly, until thick and clear. Add lemon juice, butter, and slightly beaten egg yolks and continue cooking until mixture thickens. Pour into baked pie shell and cover with meringue.

For the meringue: Beat egg whites until foamy. Add ½ teaspoon cream of tartar and beat well. Gradually add ⅓ cup sugar (about 1 tablespoon at a time) and beat until sugar is dissolved and stiff but not dry peaks form. Spread evenly over pie filling and bake at 350 degrees about 10 minutes or until meringue is a light golden brown.

CREAM PIES

As wonderful as the birthday cakes Mother made were, we absolutely cherished the cream pies Aunt Edna made for our special days.

FOR A BASIC CREAM PIE FILLING: Combine 4 tablespoons flour and ½ cup sugar in the top of a double boiler. Separate 3 eggs and set aside 2 whites for the meringue; beat the 3 yolks slightly.

Heat 1⅓ cups milk, but not quite to boiling. Stir about ¼ cup of the hot milk into the flour and sugar mixture and beat until smooth. Add the egg yolks and mix well. Add the rest of the milk gradually, stirring constantly. Add ½ teaspoon vanilla. Cook the mixture in the double boiler for about 15 minutes until it thickens, stirring constantly; then cover the double boiler to keep mixture hot.

Beat the 1 egg white until stiff; add about 1 tablespoon of the hot filling mixture to the egg white and mix well. Add about 4 or 5 more tablespoons of the filling mixture to the egg white in the same manner, then pour the egg white mixture slowly into the hot filling, stirring rapidly during the addition. Cook about 2 minutes longer. Let cool, then pour into a prebaked pie shell.

FOR THE MERINGUE: Beat the 2 egg whites until almost stiff. Add 2 tablespoons sugar and continue beating until sugar is dissolved and whites are stiff. Immediately spread over the pie filling, being careful to make sure it touches the crust around the edges. Do not spread meringue too smoothly; leave some peaks. Place pie in a 300 degree oven for 15–20 minutes until meringue browns slightly. Let cool completely before cutting and serving.

VARIATIONS

BANANA CREAM PIE — Follow the recipe for Cream Pie, but omit vanilla; stir into the cooled mixture ⅔ cup diced bananas mixed with the grated rind of ½ orange or ½ lemon.

COCONUT CREAM PIE — Add ⅔ cup shredded coconut to the Cream Pie filling. Sprinkle ⅓ plain or toasted coconut over the top of the meringue before baking.

CHOCOLATE CREAM PIE — Add 1 ½ ounces semisweet chocolate to the cold milk for the Cream Pie and heat until chocolate melts. Beat with rotary beater until well blended and proceed as with the basic Cream Pie recipe. OR, mix ⅓ cup cocoa in with the sugar, and proceed as with the basic Cream Pie recipe.

APPLE CRISP

*Few things say "autumn" better than hot apple crisp
served with vanilla ice cream.*

Arrange 4 cups sliced tart apples in a 9-inch pie pan or dish and sprinkle with 2 tablespoons lemon juice.

Mix together ½ cup all-purpose flour, ½ cup packed brown sugar, ½ teaspoon salt and 1 teaspoon cinnamon. Add ¼ cup (½ stick) butter, cold and cut into small pieces; carefully work into flour mixture with a pastry blender or fork just until mixture is crumbly. Spread mixture evenly over the apples. Bake at 375 degrees about 30 minutes or until golden. Serve hot or cold.

BREAD PUDDING

*Mother knew my passion for this dessert and made it for me
every time I came home from college.*

3 slices bread, torn into pieces

3 eggs

½ cup sugar

3 cups warm milk

1 cup raisins

1 teaspoon vanilla

½ teaspoon nutmeg

Soak bread in cold water to cover 15 minutes, then press
dry. Beat eggs and add sugar, milk, bread, raisins and vanilla
and stir to blend. Pour mixture into a buttered baking dish
and sprinkle with nutmeg. Bake at 350 degrees for about 30
minutes, or until set. Serve hot or cold.

DATE PUDDING

Thanksgiving wouldn't have been Thanksgiving without Mother's date pudding!

LET SIMMER IN A PAN:

>   2 cups boiling water
>
>   1 cup packed brown sugar
>
>   2 tablespoons butter

When sugar has completely dissolved and mixture thickens slightly, pour the mixture into a 9-by-13-inch baking pan.

IN A LARGE MIXING BOWL COMBINE AND MIX WELL:

>   ½ cup sugar
>
>   1 tablespoon butter, softened
>
>   ½ cup milk

Add 1 cup flour mixed with 1 heaping teaspoon baking powder and mix well. Add 1 teaspoon vanilla and mix well.

Fold in 1 cup chopped dates and 1 cup chopped nuts. Drop the batter by spoonfuls into the hot syrup in the baking pan. Bake at 375 degrees for 30 minutes. Serve warm with whipped cream.

PARKER HOUSE ROLLS

These were Blue Ribbon winners at both county and state fairs!

⅓ cup sugar

1 tablespoon shortening

1 teaspoon salt

1 cup boiling water

1 package active dry yeast

¼ cup lukewarm water

1 egg

4¼ cups sifted flour

Melted butter or margarine

Combine sugar, shortening, salt, and boiling water in bowl; let cool to lukewarm.

Meanwhile, sprinkle the yeast on the ¼ cup of lukewarm water; stir to dissolve. Add yeast, egg, and 1 cup flour to the water mixture; beat with electric mixer at medium speed until smooth, about 2 minutes, scraping bowl occasionally.

Gradually add enough of the remaining flour to make a soft dough that leaves the sides of the bowl. Cover and let stand 1 hour.

Turn dough out onto a lightly floured surface and roll to ½-inch thickness. Cut with floured 2 ½-inch round cutter. Brush each round with melted butter. Crease across centers of the rounds with the edge of a knife, then fold so the top half overlaps slightly. Gently press edges together. Brush tops with melted butter and place on greased baking sheet with sides touching. Let rise until doubled, about 45 minutes.

Bake at 425 degrees 15 minutes or until golden brown. Remove from baking sheet and let cool on rack. Makes 20 rolls.

HUXLEY ROLLS

An Easter dinner favorite.

1 cake yeast

1 cup sugar

1 teaspoon salt

2 cups lukewarm water

1 beaten egg

3 tablespoons melted shortening

7 cups flour

Crumble yeast into a large bowl and add the sugar, salt and water. Add the beaten egg and half (3 ½ cups) the flour. Beat until smooth. Add the melted shortening and the rest of the flour and mix to a stiff mass.

Do not turn out and knead. Cover and let rise until double in bulk. Punch down, cover, and place in the refrigerator. This dough may be used for sweet rolls or dinner rolls. Shape, let rise, and bake at 375 degrees until golden.

HUNGARIAN COFFEE CAKE

*This cake almost came apart on me on the way
to the county fair, but it didn't and I walked away
with a blue ribbon!*

MIX TOGETHER

¾ cup lukewarm milk

¼ cup sugar

1 teaspoon salt

¼ cup soft shortening

Let 1 package active dry yeast soften in ¼ cup lukewarm
water; let stand for 5 minutes, stir gently, then add to the
milk mixture. Add 1 egg and mix well.

Add 3 ½ to 3 ¾ cups sifted flour, mixing first with a spoon
and then by hand. (Note: add just enough flour to make the
dough easy to handle.)

Turn dough onto a lightly floured board, cover, and let rest
10 minutes, then knead until smooth and elastic. Shape into
a ball and place in a greased bowl. Cover with a damp cloth
and let rise until double in bulk, about 2 hours. Punch down
dough, shape into ball again and let rise once more until not
quite doubled, about 45 minutes. Punch dough down, shape,
and place on board; cover and let rest 15 minutes.

Cut dough into walnut-size pieces and form into balls. Roll
each in melted butter (about ½ cup), then roll in a mixture of
¾ cup sugar, 1 teaspoon cinnamon, and ½ cup finely chopped
nuts. Place one layer of dough balls in a greased 9-inch tube
pan so they barely touch; sprinkle with half of ½ cup raisins.
Add another layer of dough balls and sprinkle with the

remaining raisins, pressing them in slightly in the crevices. Cover with damp cloth and let rise until doubled, about 45 minutes.

Bake at 375 degrees 35–40 minutes. Immediately loosen sides with a spatula and invert on a plate so the butter-sugar mixture runs down over it. Serve by breaking pieces apart.

COOKIES

A house should have its cookie jar

For when it's half past three

And children hurrying home from school

Are hungry as can be.

There's nothing quite so splendid

In filling children up

As spicy, fluffy ginger cakes

And sweet milk in a cup.

— author unknown

CHOCOLATE CHIP OATMEAL COOKIES

The Nestle's cookie recipe went out the window when Mother discovered these outstanding wonders.

1 cup butter or shortening

¾ cup brown sugar

¾ cup granulated sugar

2 eggs, well beaten

1 teaspoon vanilla

1½ cups flour, sifted

1 teaspoon baking soda

1 teaspoon salt

2 cups quick-cooking oats

1 12-ounce package semi-sweet chocolate chips

1 cup chopped walnuts

Cream butter or shortening and the sugars. Add eggs and vanilla and mix well. Add flour, soda, and salt to the mixture and mix well. Add oats, chocolate chips, and walnuts; mix well.

Drop by teaspoonfuls onto a greased baking sheet. Bake in a 350 degree oven for 10–12 minutes or until slightly brown. Makes about 6 dozen.

HERMITS

This old German cookie recipe was extra special because we had the treats at Christmastime only.

2 cups brown sugar

1 cup (2 sticks)butter, softened

4 eggs, lightly beaten

2 teaspoons soda dissolved in a little water

5 cups unsifted flour

2 cups raisins

1 cup chopped nuts

  Grated rind of 1 orange

1 teaspoon nutmeg

1 teaspoon cinnamon

¼ cup milk

Cream butter and sugar; add eggs and soda. Add flour and remaining ingredients. Drop by teaspoonfuls onto a greased baking sheet. Bake at 350 degrees about 10 minutes or until lightly browned and "set."

SUGAR COOKIES

*Grandma McCormick's own recipe —
another family favorite.*

3 cups flour

2 teaspoons baking powder

¼ teaspoon salt

1 cup sugar

1 egg, lightly beaten

¾ cup lard, softened

¾ cup milk

3 teaspoons vanilla

Combine the flour, baking powder and salt in a large mixing bowl. Make a well in the center and add the sugar, egg and lard. Combine the milk and vanilla and slowly add to the flour mixture, stirring by hand. Shape dough into a ball and roll out to ¼-inch thickness. Sprinkle lightly with sugar and gently roll it in. Cut with cookie cutters and bake on greased pan at 400 degrees until light brown.

AUNT LILLY'S PEANUT BUTTER COOKIES

My aunt Lilly was pretty much an "eyeball" type of cook, so a written recipe from her is a treasure indeed.

- 1 cup peanut butter
- 1 cup shortening
- 1 cup granulated sugar
- 1 cup brown sugar
- 2 eggs
- 1 teaspoon baking soda dissolved in
- 1 tablespoon water
- 2½ cups flour

Combine all ingredients and mix well. Drop by teaspoonfuls on a cookie sheet. Flatten cookies by marking both ways with a fork. Bake in a 375 degree oven for 10–13 minutes.

RECIPE RESOURCES

Many of the recipes in this book are those of my mother, grandmother, and aunts. Two of my cousins compiled favorite recipes of their mother's — my aunt Midah McCormick Neal, Dad's sister — into a cookbook titled *Memories & Recipes*. Several entries are photocopies of Aunt Midah's cards and notes in her own handwriting; you can even see the smudges and smears that came from frequent use. Aunt Midah passed away in August 1996, just before the recipe book was completed, but fortunately for those of us left behind, her wonderful cooking legacy continues.

OTHER RECIPES WERE ADAPTED FROM THE FOLLOWING:
Cooking Then & Now Compiled by the Ladies of Fellowship Baptist Church, Vincennes, Indiana.

Country Fair Cookbook: Every Recipe a Blue Ribbon Winner. Elise W. Manning (Farm Journal Food Editor), ed. Garden City, NY: Doubleday & Company, Inc., 1975.

Vincennes Kitchen Secrets. Compiled by the Ladies Aid Society of St. Peters Lutheran Church, Vincennes, Indiana.

AND LAST BUT NOT LEAST, THE BOOKLETS THAT INTRODUCED ME TO BAKING:
4-H Club Baking: First Division, May 1941; Second Division, April 1944; and Fifth Division, 1948 and 1950.